Impressions of the Sahara

The wind that has heaped sand against the ocher-stoned walls in Tichit (Mauritania)
plays for a moment at lifting the veil of a local woman.

Impressions of the Sahara

JEAN-LOÏC LE QUELLEC

Photographs by
TIZIANA AND GIANNI BALDIZZONE

Flammarion

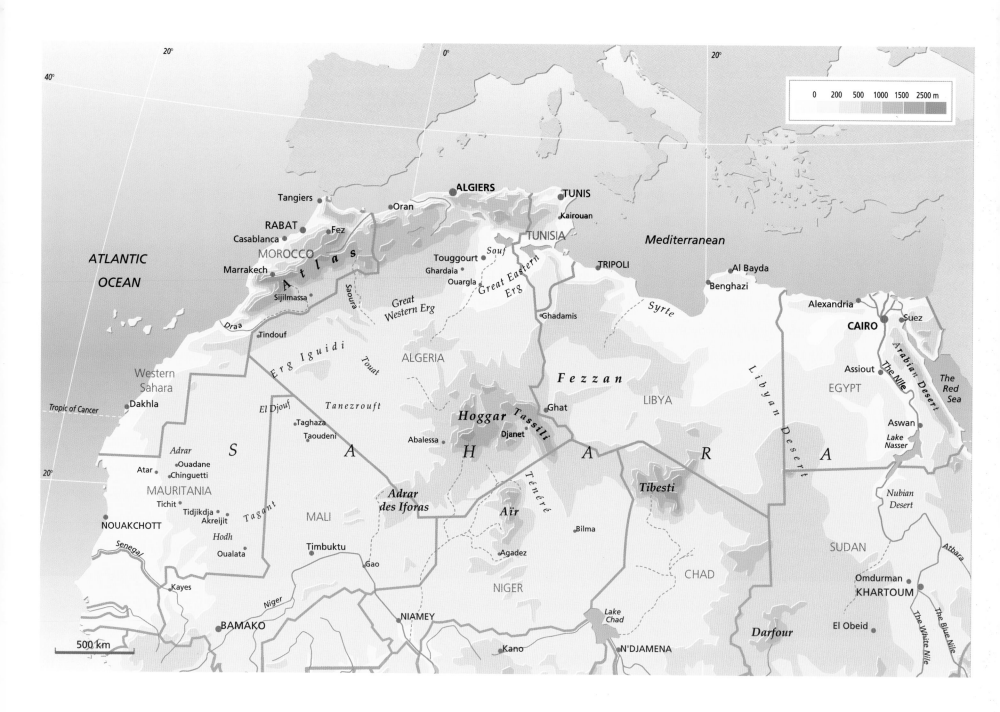

ATLANTIC

OCEAN

Tangiers

ALGIERS

TUNIS

Oran

Kairouan

RABAT

Fez

Mediterranean

Casablanca

TUNISIA

MOROCCO

Touggourt

Souf

Atlas

Ghardaia

TRIPOLI

Al Bayda

Marrakech

Ouargla

Benghazi

Great
Western Erg

Great Eastern
Erg

Sijilmassa

Saoura

Ghadamis

Syrte

Alexandria

Draa

Ghadamis

CAIRO

Suez

Tindouf

Erg Iguidi

Fezzan

Assiout

The Nile

Arabian Desert

Western
Sahara

Touat

ALGERIA

LIBYA

EGYPT

The Red
Sea

Tropic of Cancer

Dakhla

Tanezrouft

El Djouf

Ghat

Libyan Desert

Aswan

S

Hoggar

Tassili

A

R

A

Lake
Nasser

Adrar

Taghaza

Abalessa

Djanet

H

Nubian
Desert

Atar

Ouadane

Chinguetti

Taoudeni

Tibesti

20°

MAURITANIA

Adrar
des Iforas

Ténéré

SUDAN

Tichit

Tidjikdja

Akreijit

Aïr

NOUAKCHOTT

Tagant

MALI

Bilma

Athara

Hodh

Oualata

Agadez

Omdurman

Senegal

Timbuktu

CHAD

El Obeid

KHARTOUM

Kayes

Gao

NIGER

Niger

Lake
Chad

Darfour

The Blue Nile

The White Nile

500 km

BAMAKO

NIAMEY

Kano

N'DJAMENA

0   200   500   1000   1500   2500 m

40°

20°

0°

20°

CONTENTS

THE GREAT DESERT

In the great mountain ranges that cut across the heart of the Sahara, the rocks range in color from deep, velvety blacks to pastel hues of blue and mauve. In the endless sandy expanses, the palette is dominated by shades of orange and tawny ocher with pinkish undertones—from spicy saffrons and fiery oranges to mellower apricot and honey tones. In fact, the name Sahara comes from the Arabic root SHR, meaning a yellowish or tawny color. Early in the morning, before the baking sun floods the land, the dunes look slate blue. During the day, the quality of the light changes from hour to hour, taking on an infinite variety of ocher hues in the dunes and the lunar, rock-strewn landscapes known as regs. In the evening, land and sky meld in a fiery explosion of inky black and blood red, in a vision described by the French Romantic poet Alphonse de Lamartine as the "red, funereal horizon of the sandy desert."

It is worth noting that just as not all deserts are like the Sahara, not all of the Sahara can truly be called a desert. The noun "desert," a wasteland, and the verb "to desert," to abandon, both are derived from the Latin "*deserere*," to forsake or leave uninhabited, which comprises the prefix "*de-*," expressing the notion of undoing, and the verb "*serere*," to link together. In geographical terms, a desert is defined by extremely low and irregular levels of rainfall and an exceptionally dry atmosphere, leading to the erosion of the plant cover. The image of the Sahara in travel brochures, on postcards, and on the covers of books, is generally a succession of sand dunes stretching as far as the eye can see, with perhaps a palm-fringed oasis and a Bedouin herder tending his camels. And yet only one fifth of the Sahara is covered in sand dunes. The rest is dominated by stony, arid stretches of land, rocks, blocks of sandstone, cliffs, weird stone sculptures eroded by the wind over the centuries, gently sloping hills, sharp precipices, and mountains. We can only speculate that the Sahara has become synonymous with sand dunes because in a land where water is more than ever the key to life, the rippling curves of the dunes evoke the waves of an ocean lost to this harsh land forever. It is true that the dunes resemble a raging sea frozen in time, with surging peaks and deep troughs—

The Tuaregs say that the spike on the front of their saddles "sucks up the road." This tribesman is on his way to a gathering in the Aïr desert in Niger to celebrate Mouloud, the birth of the prophet Muhammad.

Preceding pages: *On the edge of the Great Western Erg in Algeria, women return from the daily chore of gathering firewood, carrying their load balanced on their heads. Behind them, the immense Kerzaz dune sprawls across the landscape like a sleeping giant.*

a "solid ocean," according to the French painter and writer Eugène Fromentin (1820–1876). Traveling along the age-old trading routes, across the rolling dunes, can sometimes feel like a long sea journey; in the evenings, it comes as a relief to set up the tents and light a camp fire—like arriving safely in port after a stormy crossing. Although the sand is nothing more than sandstone eroded into minute particles over the millennia—and that before that, the sandstone was made by unimaginable forces crushing the particles of sand until they agglomerated to form solid rock—imaginative travelers can almost hear the lapping of the waves on the sides of the ship. The French author Ernest Psichari (1883–1914) clearly had the first verses of Genesis in mind when he wrote that sand is "the primitive element, and the very substance that, in the beginning, was separated from the waters."

Travelers in the Sahara talk about "navigating" their way across the desert as they might do about a transatlantic race. The great stretches of mountainous dunes are "oceans of sand," and the camel is known as the "ship of the desert." For centuries, travelers have told how they "disembarked" safely on their arrival in the semi-arid region called the Sahel, which means "shore" in Arabic. Today, travelers are equipped with the latest four-wheel-drive vehicles and Global Positioning Systems—the equivalent of the compass and sextant used to plot the ship's position by the stars in centuries past. Here and there, where a vehicle has come to grief, all that remains is a wreck, the skeleton of the car, like the bones of an animal picked clean by scavengers. Philippe Diolé, a respected biologist, described "the stranded truck, gnawed by rust, and the boat caught on a sandbank, tried beyond endurance, reeling, on its flank. In the solitude of the ocean, in the silence of the erg, the same anonymity, the same sadness of things dying rather than dead, abandoned without hope to the sands of the deeps, the sands of the wind." The inhabitants of Ouadane and Chinguetti still call the caravan that takes sacks of salt to Senegal for trade *el-gareb*, the boat. When, in 1962, the explorer and naturalist Théodore Monod came across a load of cowry shells and brass ingots left behind by a caravan that had run into difficulties, he wrote of how the discovery reminded him of the flotsam washed up after a shipwreck.

If the Sahara is an ocean of sand, then the oases are the islands. Herodotus wrote that one of them, seven days' journey from Thebes, was known to the Greeks as the "island of the blessed." To extend the analogy, we could see cities like Ghadamis as ports of call or safe harbors for the caravans on a journey as dangerous as any deep-sea trawler's. Caught in a sandstorm in Djanet, in 1950, Philippe Diolé wrote "the sand-filled wind has forced its way into the oasis like the waves of a stormy ocean force their way into a port." Every traveler—sailor and desert explorer alike—dreads storms. No mariner's story is complete without an episode recounting the terrors of a storm at sea, the roaring cyclone lifting mountains of glassy water to pound down on the ship, cracking the timbers and snapping the solid trunks of the masts like matchsticks. Likewise, every tale of exploits in the Sahara recounts the mortal peril of the blinding, stinging wind that blows up out of nowhere in a matter of seconds, in a world where to lose sight of the path means a slow and lingering death by thirst. The desert winds—the khamsin, the ghibli, and the simoom—fully deserve the fearful respect in which they are held by the desert dwellers.

The term simoom—meaning a hot, dry, desert wind—comes from the Arabic word *samum*, or "poisoned." The fifteenth sura of the Koran tells how Allah used the simoom to

create jinn. The Tunisians, Libyans, and Egyptians also say that the ghibli, the Arabic term for "southern," often brings a sandstorm in its wake. In 1933, Charles D'Agostino described it thus: "At dawn, we are awoken by a gust of the ghibli. It mews, bellows, and roars in turn, terrifyingly, while from the farthest reaches of the Sahara, suffocating blasts of furnace heat and blinding clouds of sand arrive at an incredible speed."

The ghibli is a hot wind that blows from the southern reaches of the desert, bringing with it tons of sand. However, its effects and the danger it represents have generally been greatly exaggerated by writers who have never set foot in the desert and who have never experienced a true sandstorm. The earliest of these tall travelers' tales date back to antiquity.

In 1939, the amateur geographer Diego Brosset wrote ironically of the professional topographers who, when they came to stretches of sand (here, on the border between Algeria and Libya), stopped exploring and just colored the map yellow. He added that if ever they dared venture into the dunes, they were often astonished to discover the diversity of life forms that survived there.

It was common practice for travelers to "embroider" their story, often drawing on geographical sources by previous explorers that were themselves far from reliable. Writers were expected to build on the stories invented by their predecessors as a way of proving that they had indeed visited the places they claimed to have seen. (One legend of a tribe in central Africa with tails proved especially long-lived: it was still hotly disputed by scientists in the nineteenth century). The fifth-century B.C.E., Greek historian Herodotus includes in the fourth book of his *Histories* a section on the tribes living in the Libyan desert. He recounts the legend of the Psylli tribe, said to have vanished from the face of the earth when they tried to defeat a sandstorm (it was customary in certain regions to attempt to fight the storms, as it was believed that they harbored evil spirits).

The neighbours of the Nasamones are the Psylli—but they no longer exist. There is a story which I repeat as the Libyans tell it: that the south wind dried up the water in their storage tanks, so that they were left with none whatever, as their territory lies wholly within the Syrtis. Upon this they held a council, and having unanimously decided to declare war on the south wind, they marched out to the desert, where the wind blew and buried them in sand. The whole tribe was wiped out, and the Nasamones occupied their former domain.[1]

The Sahara is an ocean where, instead of salt spray, the winds blow up clouds of sand. When travelers lose their way in a storm, they can drown in the sand that stings their eyes, blocks their nose, chokes up their mouth, and desiccates their flesh. In 1883, the explorer Henri Brosselard wrote:

In the heart of this tornado of dust that the wind is blowing in all directions, the convoy can only advance with great difficulty. We are all suffering, man and beast alike. The camels and horses turn their heads aside from the sandstorm that is blinding them; sometimes they stop, as if they are suffocating. Our faces are covered by a burnoose, our eyes are half-closed, we can't open our mouths without the sand blowing in. . . . The burning sand, whipped violently by the wind, sticks to everything in its path, and any horseman who has not taken the precaution of wrapping all his water gourds in a thick layer of *drinn* [a plant that grows in the Sahara] or who lays them on the ground without sufficiently sheltering them, will find the sand has sucked or drawn the water through the goatskin it is kept in, until it has all gradually evaporated. How many travelers have thus perished, their bones hidden by the sand of the dunes?

This haunting fear is echoed by Eugène Fromentin in *A Summer in the Sahara*: "I am resigned to watching the sand pile up on my trunks, my boxes, and spreading all over me, as if I were in danger of being buried alive."

The Countess Z., who wrote an account of her adventures driving across the Sahara in 1933, also gave a graphic—if rather fanciful—description of her experience: "Shut in the car, we heard the wind, which was continually increasing in intensity, throwing the desiccated bones of the numerous camel carcasses strewn along the road against the windows." The great traveler Théodore Monod is said to have been most amused by her wildly extravagant claims. Monod was one of the twentieth century's major specialists in desert environments, a profound thinker and passionate in his defense of the natural world. He died, aged ninety-eight, in 2000.

Preceding pages:
Left: *The wind whistles through a narrow passage between two rocks in the cliff face that divides the Tagant from the sandy desert (Mauritania).*
Right: *The wind is omnipresent, whipping up the sand, tirelessly sculpting, hollowing, and smoothing the rocks and cliffs. Taoujaft Guelta (water hole), Mauritania.*

Above: *A desert horizon and a pyramid—not in Egypt, but in the Erg Admer, Algeria, where these shapes are born of the ceaseless dialogue of the wind and the sand. Pyramid-shaped live (i.e. shifting) dunes like this are known as* ghourd *in the central Sahara, and* gherd *or* ghord *in Mauritania.*

The modern Tuareg poet Hawad wrote, "Like the vocal cords of a cobra sucking the venom up from its hips, I stretch myself." The sweeping curves of the dunes in the Libyan Desert are one of the most inhospitable places on earth.

THE STORY OF THE OASES

I n April 1352 (753 A.H., After Hegira in the Islamic calendar), the Arabic traveler Ibn Battuta, on his way from Marrakech to Mali via Sijilmassa and the Taghaza salt mines, arrived within sight of Oualata, in those days called Iwalatan. In his account of his travels, he noted that it was customary to pay a *takshif*, or scout, to enter the town ahead of the caravan, bearing letters addressed to friends living at the oasis "so that they rent homes in readiness and come to meet the caravan with water at a distance of four days' journey from the oasis." Those not fortunate enough to have friends at Iwalatan had no choice but to trust their luck to finding an accommodating merchant to house them and furnish them with water. Ibn Battuta laid great emphasis on the danger of such desert crossings, writing "in this desert, there are no tracks or trails: there is only sand, blown away by the wind." He added that there was also a danger from the numerous demons who lived in the desert, who delighted in tormenting the unfortunate *takshifs*, tempting them from the path and leading them astray to certain death.

Ibn Battuta's writings echo the age-old belief that sees the desert as the very definition of a desolate wilderness, inhabited only by savage beasts and demons. This belief is as old as the Bible. "Who led thee through that great and terrible wilderness, wherein were fiery serpents, and scorpions, and drought, where there was no water?" (Deuteronomy 8:15). Marco Polo took up the image in 1298 in his depiction of the desert of China, in his celebrated *Description of the World*, also called the *Book of Marvels*: "The people take it as a manifest truth that in the said desert [Lop] there dwell a number of spirits that produce great and astonishing illusions to make voyagers perish . . . and many people, not being forewarned of these spirits, die a terrible death." Ibn Battuta adds to the tale that when a

Many Saharan oases have narrow covered streets to protect the inhabitants from the burning sun. Kerzaz, Algeria.

Preceding pages: *The town of Ghardaia (Algeria) was founded in 1053 by Ibadite Berbers who wished to settle away from the great trade routes. Today, the town is home to some twenty thousand people.*

takshif is led astray by the demons, "the inhabitants of Iwalatan know nothing of the caravan, which thus perishes entirely or for the most part."

Ibn Battuta also noted how astonished he was to discover that the guide leading his caravan was "blind in one eye, and the other was diseased, [but that] he knew the route better than anyone." This is one of the earliest mentions of the quasi-legendary theme of the blind guide, which has featured regularly in Saharan travel narratives ever since. Jean Gabus, writing in the 1960s, told how Mokhtar, a famous guide in the Tagjakant region, "could identify the regions of the desert by their smell, taste, and touch, letting the sand flow through his fingers. To be even more certain, he would close his blind eyes, saying 'You have to be blind to know.'" A legend recounts that the oasis town of Tichit was founded by the blind guide al-Amin bel-Hajj, who traveled with a group of companions from lands in the east. Each day, he would choose their direction by sniffing a pinch of sand. After a few days, his fellow travelers began to doubt in his abilities. One morning, one of the travelers tried to trick the guide by presenting him with a fistful of sand he had kept from the day before. Al-Amin bel-Hajj was able to tell straight away that the sand was not fresh, and after that, his companions had no further qualms in entrusting him with their lives.

To this day, in isolated oasis towns, the locals speak with admiration of the old men who, although almost completely blind, have no difficulty in leading a caravan to places rarely visited. One such legendary guide, still remembered with awe in Libya, was Karnafuda. It is said he could tell where sand had come from just by touching it. The Libyans say *ya'rifah bi-l-ramla*—he knew the Sahara by its sand. These legends recounting the exploits of blind guides are derived from the age-old theme of the blind visionary whose inner eye developed to compensate for the earthly handicap. In other words, the inner eye makes up for the loss of ordinary vision. The legend has proved particularly tenacious in the Sahara, where the human gaze can often see uninterrupted for dozens of miles.

Oases, the ports on the ocean of the Saharan sands, can often be seen from miles away; there can be many weary hours of travel between the moment when the town is first sighted and the moment of arrival. On the regs, under the crushing heat of the sun, the only way to make any headway is to carry on doggedly putting one foot in front of the other, following the tracks of the person in front, trying not to stumble on the loose scree, not wasting any energy speaking. Gradually, over the course of time, a *mrira*, or path, is traced between the rocks. When several *mrair* (the plural of *mrira*) are created along the same route, they form a *mejbed*, or road, a silent witness to the countless thousands of travelers who have taken the same route through the perils of the desert. It is very moving to retrace the footsteps of these generations of traders and explorers. At certain points along the route, the feet of the men and their beasts of burden have worn a groove in a slab of rock, forming a channel so smooth that the stone sparkles in the sun. The rock has been polished by the bare feet and leather sandals of countless travelers in an infinitely gradual yet irreversible process of erosion. I am reminded of the tale of the stony outcrop worn away to nothing over the millennia by an immortal bird of prey that briefly wipes its beak on the rock after devouring its kill. Another legend tells of a bronze ball worn down to nothing by a swallow that brushes it with the tip of its wing as it flies past once a century.

These legends symbolize a world where change occurs so slowly that time seems to stand still. This is the story of the dunes that are constantly shifting, and yet eternally present. It is the story of the world's languages, which seem set in stone, yet are constantly changing—and some of which become extinct.

Although language is constantly evolving, some words are common to many languages. One of these is the term for a watering hole in the desert, and the town that has grown up around it. The word is *oasis* in English, French, Spanish, Estonian, and Russian; *oásis* in Portuguese; *oasi* in Italian and modern Greek; *Oase* in German and Dutch; *oaza* in Romanian and Polish; *oas* in Swedish; *oázis* in Hungarian; and *oashisu* in Japanese—the list goes on. Given the linguistic dominance of Arabic in the Saharan region, it seems paradoxical that the Arabic term for an oasis, *wahat,* has only passed into Persian and Turkish (*vaha*). In fact, in Arabic, oases are almost always referred to by the name of the town, so that travelers say they are going to Ghardaia or Tamentit, or that three days' travel will

Near the marketplace in Ghardaia, the sun lights up the arcades, shifting the shadows that provide a modicum of protection for men and animals alike.

bring them in sight of al-Kufra. On leaving an oasis, they say they are "going into the Sahara," an expression which also means to lead a nomadic lifestyle.

In fact, the word is simply derived from the ancient Greek town of Oasis. In his description of the conquest of Egypt by the Persians, Herodotus writes how the conquering army set out from Thebes, "traveling with guides; it is evident that they reached the town of Oasis." The word took on its current meaning of a dwelling place in inhospitable desert surroundings in the first century B.C.E., when the great Greek geographer Strabo (c. 64 B.C.E.–c. 24 C.E.) compared the desert to a panther skin dotted with oases. The Greeks had borrowed the word from the ancient Egyptians. It figures in hieroglyphic texts dating from the sixth dynasty (c. 2345 B.C.E.), and is thus one of the oldest attested place names in the world.

Oases are defined by two characteristics: the presence of water in sufficient quantities to grow plants, and permanent dwellings. The inhabitants of the oases gave up their wandering lifestyle generations ago for the security of a fixed abode. The desert nomads live in tents of camel, sheep, and goat hair. When they arrive in an oasis after a long, perilous journey, it seems like paradise to be in a place with such an abundance of water after the privations of the desert. But soon they set off once again on their endless journey.

It would be wrong to see the opposing lifestyles of the inhabitants of the oasis and the nomads as evidence of a difference of ethnicity or mentality, or of an "ancestral urge" to

wander, which is nothing more than a romanticized fiction of the nomad lifestyle that has gained currency in the West. The reasons why certain tribes opt for a nomadic lifestyle are neither ethnic nor mystical. In fact, in its narrowest sense, the word "nomad" (from the Greek *nemein*, to lead animals to pasture) refers only to pastoral societies. Herodotus distinguished between *aroteres*, or plowmen, and *nomades*, or shepherds. Genesis 4:20 defines nomads as "such as dwell in tents, and . . . such as have cattle." In the Islamic world view, land is classed as *Dar al-Islam*, or domain of Islam, divided into the *blad al-makhzen*, or "civilized" land on which tax is paid, and the *blad al-Siba*, the "insubordinate land," consisting of expanses of wilderness beyond Islamic control. The Islamic notion of *'umran* or civilization thus encompasses the opposing lifestyles of nomadic tribes (*badawa*) relying directly on natural resources for their daily needs, and a sedentary lifestyle (*hadhara*) where natural resources undergo transformation before consumption, and where society is thus divided into workers and a ruling aristocratic class.

It would be just as incorrect to consider oases as miracles of nature, corners mysteriously spared by the process of creeping desertification that has gradually taken over much of northern Africa over the past four thousand years. In fact, there are thousands of springs and wells throughout the Sahara that have not developed into oases. Several factors need to come together for a permanent settlement to grow up around a well: the site must be able to supply the trading caravans with sufficient water and food, and be able to provide

Immense, burnt-orange dunes, with sloping flanks or gentle curves, tower over an army of angular black pillars and rock formations that resemble ruined forts or ghost towns. Two facets of the Algerian desert in the Tin-Merzouga region.

a marketplace where the traders can carry out their business in privacy and, just as importantly, in safety. Oasis towns generally have a series of fortifications to protect against raiders, such as city walls with gated entrances, twisting passages, and a labyrinth of streets. The *ksour*, or fortified Berber villages, are real fortresses. It is worth noting that the emblematic plant of the oases, the palm tree, was introduced by man and cannot survive in the extreme desert conditions without constant care.

All in all, the oases owe more to man than they do to nature. The five towns of Bou Nouara, el-Atteuf, Beni Isguene, Melika, and Ghardaia in Algeria are a fine example of this. The five towns, strung out over some five miles (nine kilometers) were founded in the eleventh century on hills overlooking the M'zab Wadi, a barren valley. The first inhabitants were Berbers who finally settled here after they had been forced to flee from Kairouan, Tahart, and the Ouargla region because they were followers of the Ibadite sect, deemed heretical by the Sunni majority. The new inhabitants came to be known as M'zabites or Mozabites, meaning "those who live in the M'zab region." Paradoxically, it was the very harshness of the environment that led them to settle here, as only in an isolated and inhospitable region like this could they be free to practice their austere Khariji faith. The M'zabite oases, far from the traditional trading routes, flourished thanks to their plantations of nearly three hundred thousand date palms and their thriving markets, which eventually brought them to the attention of the trading caravans. They were a convenient trading post for caravans on their way to the great oases in Fezzan and southern Mauritania. For centuries, the routes across the Sahara hardly varied. Caravans would set out from the three great centers in the north, Sijilmassa, Touat, and Ouargla, on the frontier between the Sahara and the Atlas Mountains. These three towns were the main point of entry into the desert for goods shipped into the ports on the Mediterranean coast. The major trading routes crossed the desert to three towns on the southern fringes of the desert—Blad al-Sudan, "the black country," as Arab writers called the southern reaches of the Sahara. Once they had arrived safely in the three towns of Timbuktu, Gao, and Agadez, the goods would be sold on all over Africa. The journey took the traders across the Tropic of Cancer, via the salt mines of Taghaza, Taoudeni, and Abalessa. There were also two lesser trading routes, one to the east from Tripoli to Bilma via Ghadamis and Ghat in Fezzan, and the other to the west, from Sijilmassa to Audaghost (the fourth capital of the kingdoms of Sudan) via Tindouf, Atar, Chinguetti, and Tidjikdja. Another route led from Tidjikdja to Timbuktu via Tichit and Oualata, before heading back to the north. Traders frequently took a different route to return home.

Obviously, the oases that lay along these trading routes had a greater chance of prosperity than more isolated sites, although they were entirely dependent on the economy of the region as a whole and on the caravans that passed through in particular. This meant that they were badly hit when European traders discovered it was more profitable to sail to the Gulf of Guinea to plunder the untold riches offered by West Africa, such as gold, ivory—and slaves.

Since climate change has meant the Sahara has been spreading over the last few centuries, travelers are entirely dependent on dromedaries to carry their water gourds, and on

finding regular supplies of the precious liquid along their route. It was—and is—literally a matter of life and death. The importance of water in the collective consciousness of desert dwellers is clearly illustrated by the richness of the vocabulary in this field. It is well known that the Inuits have dozens of words for types of snow; likewise, the Tuaregs have an astonishingly specialized vocabulary for what in English can only be referred to as a well or a spring. *Abankor* means a temporary well, where the sand must be scraped from the surface to reach the water; *achgig* refers to a similar sort of well, but slightly deeper. *Tilma* means a straightforward hole dug in the sand to collect water, *tirs* means a hole at least six feet (two meters) in depth, *afadyar* is a newly dug well, *aguelman* a natural watering hole, *atafala* a large pond at the surface that does not need to be dug for, *amyour* a well dug on the same spot as a previous water hole, *archan* a temporary well whose walls are not reinforced, and which lies in a wadi or dried-up pond. *Tanout* means the same sort of well without reinforced walls, but with a pulley system, in a garden.

Some wells that lay along busy paths or even at the crossroads of major trading routes or near important towns were destined to become trading centers in their own right. Over time, a few huts would be built, and vegetable patches scratched out of the sand. In fact, little is known about the origins of the oases, although many have their own traditional tales recounting the foundation of the town—myths in which water always plays a large part.

One such tale is told about the town of Chinguetti, said to have been founded in 776. The town suffered a gradual decline in its fortunes over the centuries. The legend tells how the son of the ruler of Abweir, Yahya Lkhrami, murdered one of his cousins. The punishment for such a crime was death; but because Yahya Lkhrami was of noble birth, he was exiled instead. He left Abweir and set up camp in Chinguetti, which some linguists claim means "the horse spring." There he became friends with a saintly hermit called Mhammed Khrelli. The two friends were later joined by two other men from Abweir, Amar Ibni

The towns of Beni-Isguen (in the foreground), Melika, and Ghardaia were built on the flanks of the M'zab Wadi (Algeria), which gave its name to their inhabitants, the M'zabites or Mozabites.

Facing page: *The houses lining the narrow streets of the ancient Mozabite oasis of Beni-Isguen are often painted in delicate pastel shades that are restful for the eyes after the glaring light of the sun.*

In the sixth century, the poet Imru'al-Qays sang of "the nights when, submitting to your pleasure, Selma stretched out the white, straight dune of her teeth and her neck of white light." The curves of the vast Tin-Merzouga dune in Algeria seem to echo the imagery of the great Arab poet.

The ripples on the surface of the dunes evoke the landscape as seen from an airplane.

and Ideijir. The four men decided to found a new town, with Amar Ibni as the mason, Ideijir the carpenter, Yahya the guard, and Khrelli the imam and *qadi*, or magistrate. They built a mosque, and little by little, the inhabitants of Abweir left their homes to come and live in the new oasis. After forty years, Abweir had ceased to exist, and Chinguetti was flourishing. Houses with red stone walls were springing up from the pink sand, forming a striking contrast with the bright green foliage of the date palms. Although the original mosque is long gone, it is tempting to imagine the young town growing up round the mosque that stands in the center of the town today, its minaret towering thirty feet (ten meters) over the surrounding houses. Each corner of the tower is topped with a stick holding aloft an ostrich egg, a symbol of hope.

Although opinions are divided over the derivation of the name Chinguetti—not all experts agree it means "the horse spring"—the traditional etymology does correspond with characteristics noted by linguists in folk tales from many nomadic cultures. It is thus entirely possible that the name of this oasis comes from a nomadic language.

The inhabitants of another famous oasis, Ghadamis, tell how their town grew up around a remarkable spring called "the mare's spring." The tale goes that one day, Sidi 'Oqba al-Badri, a companion of the Prophet Muhammad, stopped here for a rest with his followers. His mare was dying of thirst. It pawed the ground with its hoof, and from the sand there sprang an Artesian well that in time filled a pond measuring ninety feet (thirty meters) in diameter. As ever, the town grew up around the water supply. In an Arabic manuscript dated 7 Muharrem 1181 A.H. (June 6, 1767), held in the French national library in Paris, a certain Mustafa Khuja ben Qasim el-Macri writes how a merchant by the name of el-Ensari from Ghadamis explained to him that a local tradition held that the town was founded by Nimrod the hunter, son of Canaan, son of Shem, son of Noah, son of

The variety of colors and tones found in the Saharan landscape is often reflected in desert architecture, as in these ancient buildings in Oualata, Mauritania, once a major halt on the Saharan trading routes.

Adam. The legend told that the Aïn el-Fares spring ("the horseman's spring") sprang forth under the hoof of a mare belonging to one of Nimrod's fellow travelers.

In the thirteenth century, the Arab geographer Zakariya ben Muhammad ben Mahmud Abu Tahya al-Qaswini noted down a similar legend relating to the Kawar region, including the oases to the north of Lake Chad. He wrote:

It is a region of the lands of the Sudan to the south of Fezzan, where Aïn el-Fares (the horse's spring) lies. It is told that 'Oqba ben 'Amir traveled as far as Kawar and carried out many raids in the region. Exhausted by thirst, he and his troops nearly perished. So 'Oqba stood up to pray, threw himself down on the ground twice, crying out the name of the Most Holy One, when suddenly he saw his horse pawing the sand and clearing a rock from which water was flowing. The horse began to drink. On seeing this, 'Oqba called his companions who dug in the sand and were able to refresh themselves. Since then, this spring has been known as the horse's spring.

As we have seen, the founding myths of the oasis towns frequently refer to the miraculous discovery of a spring by a horse pawing at the sand, thus saving a group of travelers from dying of thirst. It is significant that the myths always refer to horses, and not to animals more commonly associated with the Sahara, such as camels, as this indicates that the foundation myths are no older than the introduction of horses to the desert environment. It is also important to note that the myths also always refer to Arab, not African, travelers from Nimrod (who is mentioned on several occasions in the Koran) to 'Oqba, companion of the Prophet and conqueror of the Sahara. Yet it is difficult to avoid drawing an obvious parallel between these myths and the Greek legend that recounts how the Hippocrene fountain welled up beneath the hooves of Pegasus, given the identical etymological derivations of the names of the springs (in ancient Greek, *hippos* means horse and *krene* spring). The myths in fact tell us more about the spread of Arab culture and of the Islamic faith in this part of the world than about the history of the oasis towns. The earliest inhabitants of the oases seem to have adopted the myths of the dominant Arab culture, borrowed in turn from the ancient Greeks, to explain how prosperous towns came to be founded in such inhospitable climes.

Of course, the oases owed their prosperity less to the miracle of a horse seeking out an invisible spring than to the patient labor of generations of local inhabitants who had no choice but to find a reliable water supply, and then tame it, protect it, channel it, and store it, using techniques tried and tested by desert dwellers for thousands of years. They used the most efficient and sparing methods to irrigate the vegetable patches they had scratched out from the desert sands, and which represented the main food supply of the oasis.

One of the most widespread techniques, still in use today, is to bring water up from the water table lying deep below the surface by using a *shaduf* or well sweep, or with a bucket and winch system, powered by hand or by beasts of burden. Another technique, more rarely found, is digging down to reach the water rather than bringing it up to the surface. This is the technique used in the Souf region in Algeria, for example, where the locals have dug immense excavations, or *ghout*. Palm trees are planted in the bottoms of the *ghout*, where their roots are closer to the water table. A third technique relies on a vast network of underground galleries, or *foggara*, where the water collects. The researcher Pietro Laureano argues the case for distinguishing between oases in wadis, ergs, and *sabkhahs*, since the way the locals use the scarce water resources available to them depends on the nature of the land. Wadi oases lie along dry riverbeds, where the locals tend their gardens and palm tree plantations. Well sweeps (called *khottara* in Morocco) are placed along the old course of the river, and the habitations are generally strung out along the banks of the wadi. Oases in ergs (from the Arabic *'erg*, meaning a landscape of dunes) lie in the mountainous Saharan dunes, leading a constant battle against the invasion of the desert sands by creating artificial dunes called *afreg*. They dig vast craters in the sand and plant their crops in the bottom, closer to the water table, so that they need practically no irrigation at all. The Arabic word *sabkhah* refers to dried-up lakes. *Sabkhah* oases are towns built on the shores of these lakes. Because the ground is heavily impregnated with salt, the water is drained into underground chambers through a network of *foggara*. The technology of this system is so perfectly adapted to the specific difficulties of the terrain that experts see it as evidence of the highly advanced knowledge and application of hydraulic engineering developed by some Saharan cultures.

In most places, these traditional techniques have fallen out of use, to be replaced by more modern, technology-based solutions. In some towns, the traditional techniques are

The steep slope at the crest of the dune formed by the wind is called a sif, *from the Arabic term for a saber, as it often imitates the curve of a scimitar blade. Erg Medjehebat, north of Ahaggar, Algeria.*

still in place, but have undergone spectacular improvements. However, in both of these cases, the result has been the same: an extremely rapid change in the local environment. Nowadays, deep wells are being sunk all over the Sahara, and an artificial river has even been created to take water from the Libyan Sahara to the Mediterranean coast. These major advances have their drawbacks. Increasingly, the water being drawn is tainted with salt as the irreplaceable reserves of fossil water are used up, and the chemical composition of the soil is being altered to the detriment of the plant life. These are the unfortunate consequences of the rush to put technologies into place before all the ramifications of their use have been fully explored. It seems as if the age-old dream of reclaiming the desert for agriculture is not as straightforward as it seemed just a few years ago.

Sadly, it must also be recognized that the traditional economies of the oasis towns are no longer viable. The merchants can no longer hope to make a living as their ancestors did, by controlling the trade along the caravan routes in gold, ivory, and other precious commodities, including slaves. It might be thought that until twentieth-century travel opened up the desert, the oases were isolated settlements, cut off from the world except for the occasional passage of trading caravans. In fact, this was far from being the case: the oases prospered because they held economic sway over extremely wide areas. It should also be said that oasis societies traditionally acquired much of their wealth from the labor of a category of workers generally considered to be an inferior species. From this point of view, the advent of a more democratic age should be welcomed.

These days, the oases are shadows of their former selves. The palm plantations are neglected and thirsty, the gardens overgrown, the streets choked with sand, and the superb

traditional architecture is crumbling away, replaced with rather hideous concrete blocks. The satellite dishes on the side of many of the houses give a clue as to the dreams and aspirations of the modern inhabitants of these ancient oasis towns. The young people are increasingly convinced that their future lies in the cities rather than in these dusty streets. Conversely, wealthy Westerners have begun to see the magic of the desert as an instant cure for the ills of modern life—stress, noise, and pollution. If their societies are to survive, the inhabitants of the oases will have to find new ways of living in harmony with the desert, in the towns that generations of travelers saw as earthly paradises. The ancient Persian word *pairi-daeza*, or garden, was borrowed by both Arabic and English to mean the ideal, heavenly garden; the Arabic term *jenna* refers both to oasis gardens and to the Muslim paradise.

Is modern society truly incompatible with the centuries-old traditions of the oases? Or will the oasis towns manage to adapt to today's world and the advent of a global economy by offering wealthy Western tourists a once-in-a-lifetime desert experience, a two-week taste of an ancestral society that it takes a lifetime to explore?

Maybe, in a few hundred years' time, a poet will once again catch a glimpse of a young girl wrapped in an azure veil just before she slips through a heavy wooden door in a ocher wall, and be inspired to echo these lines by Arthur Rimbaud:

I know it is Thou, who in this place,
Minglest thine almost Saharan blue![2]

The wind creates similar curves on a much smaller scale in a fine example of the fractal effect. Whatever the scale, the sand must obey the laws of physics, and cannot build up a slope at an angle of more than thirty-three degrees.

In the Saoura region of Algeria, the sharp lines and blocks of color of this modern house make a bold contrast with the curves of the dune, forming a striking abstract composition.

31

Geologists read the history of the desert in its sands.
Like snowflakes, no two samples of sand are ever identical.

Following pages: *A series of archways in a long-abandoned building in an oasis in the Saoura region of Algeria (left) echo the natural arches of the rocks in the Makrouga massif in Mauritania (right). The wind shrieking through the arches is said to be the voices of the* Kel al-Souf, *spirits of the void, or jinn.*

THE SCULPTED
HOUSES OF AGADEZ

Sensitive town planning, carefully built houses, and a harmonious architectural style are generally the fruit of human experience adapted over generations to the specific characteristics of the local environment and to the region's history and culture. The use of local building materials is normally a means of ensuring a harmonious combination of colors and textures, while builders working with traditional materials can be relied on to know the simplest and most effective ways to put them to best use. At first glance, it might seem that some Saharan towns have adopted a generally long, low building style in unwitting imitation of their natural surroundings, and that the arches and cupolas are inspired by the shape of the dunes. Yet this is far from the truth. Although some travelers have been known to speculate in an idle moment that traditional architecture is generally inspired by the surrounding landscape, this is clearly not the case: if it were so, Gothic spires would be found in mountainous regions more than in the plains, and minarets more often on *jebels* (hills) than *dhars* (plateaus). It is far more accurate and instructive to realize that traditional construction techniques and designs are a reflection of the hopes and aspirations of the society that is to live in the houses and work, study, and pray in the buildings. The life span of a new building depends less on the malleability of the clay, the density of the sandstone, and the solidity of the schist slabs, than on the cohesion of the society for which it is planned, the weight of tradition behind the architect, and the symbolic role of the building.

Many authors have written on the subject of traditional Mauritanian desert architecture, nearly always trying to pin down architectural influences in the surrounding environment, or, failing that, further afield—in the countries of North Africa and the Mediterranean basin, in the Middle East, or even in Rhodesia via Portuguese interests in

The banco façades of homes in Agadez, Niger, are often decorated with raised geometric patterns (above and facing).

Preceding pages: *Multicolored decorations in a room of the Baker's House.*

the two regions. Others tirelessly seek out echoes of past civilizations—Hispanic, Moorish, Byzantine, Yemenite, and Assyrian influences have all been claimed.

There is some truth in Théodore Monod's case for dividing Mauritanian desert architecture into three principal styles. The first, centered around Tichit-Akreijit, Chinguetti, and Ouadane, uses squared-off stones and earth mortar but no clay coating, and the lintels are of stone. The second, found in the Adrar-Tagant region, is similar to the first but for the use of wall coatings and wooden lintels, while the third is based on the use of clay, for example the buildings in Oualata. There are indeed frequent traces of Berber and Sudanese influences, in the use of dry-stone walls and clay (*toub*, adobe, or banco), respectively.

It is perfectly feasible that sub-Saharan influences played a part in a whole facet of Moorish *ksar* architecture (*ksar*, plural *ksour*, means a fortress or stronghold), given that prior to the seventeenth century, the language spoken in the region was Azer, a local variety of Soninke (spoken in what is now Ghana) influenced by Berber. Azer was still the lingua franca in Oualata, Tichit, and Ouadane in the mid-nineteenth century. The slaves who arrived in the region from the Sahel (the southern boundary of the desert), who played a major role in introducing agricultural methods such as date palm plantations, and who must also have been present in the building trade, represented another possible source of influence.

All of these points are perfectly true. And yet, whether the architecture was purely local or open to outside influence—from near or far—it remains the case that establishing patterns of influence is in this case less important than recognizing the significance of the fact that the local builders took up a style and made it their own. For example, each house has its own inner courtyard—not, as might be thought, because of the climate, but because in the Islamic faith, the first and most important house was the one built by Muhammad in Medina for his family and as a meeting place for his followers. The courtyard of the houses in Agadez is there as a reminder of the home's dual function as a safe haven from persecution and as a place of learning. Oleg Grabar, a specialist in the history of Islamic art, writes that good architecture is always an invitation to behave in a certain manner. It is certainly true that people use architecture to shape their daily lives, from their relationship with the deity in their places of worship to more mundane activities such as eating, sleeping, chatting, or even debating some arcane point of traditional prosody. In short, architecture is one of life's ornaments, and part of the spice of daily life.

Sometimes, the names of places are evidence of the complex fabric of history. Agadez, the principal town in the Aïr desert, is a fine example of this. Some researchers have claimed that the town's name is derived from a Berber term for a fortress, *agadir*. However, it has been demonstrated that this term derives from the Semitic root GDR, connoting strength, while the name Agadez, pronounced *Egedeh*, *Egedesh*, or *Egedez* by the Tuaregs, in fact comes from the Berber verb *egdez*, to forgather. The name Agadez thus suggests a meeting place for a large number of people. This interpretation of the name accords with the evidence of an early traveler, the Arab geographer Leo Africanus, who noted in his *Description of Africa*, written in the early sixteenth century, that the inhabitants of Agadez "are almost all foreign merchants." It is believed that the town's earliest inhabitants, the Magadezas, were Tuaregs, who only owned shops there, some of which are still standing today. The oldest buildings in the town are thought to date from the fifteenth century. As is often the case, the truth about

The geometric forms above are functional as well as decorative: they help keep the rooms cool.

the town's foundation is still a matter of dispute, but one thing is certain: the site was inhabited long before the spread of Islam to this part of the world, and the town owed its development to its location at the crossroads of two major trading routes, from Tripoli to Kano, and from Cairo to Gao, and then on to Timbuktu. Moreover, it is interesting to note that the route linking the great trading centers of Timbuktu, Gao, and Agadez was the furthest south that camels could be used as beasts of burden, and at the same time the northern limit of tsetse fly infestation, a plague that affected a vast zone covering much of Africa. The route traces the border between two worlds. Agadez, with an average rainfall of eight inches (two hundred millimeters) in a good year—four times more than in Iferouane—was also a major stopping point for the *Aïri*, the great caravan of several thousand camels that crossed the desert every year to Bilma to bring back precious commodities such as dates and salt. The names of certain districts of Agadez—Ghadamis, Gao-Gao—refer to the place of origin of the local community, while others are a reminder of the town's Songhai origins— Bangoutara, Ogouberi, Tanouberi, Youbboutara.

Leo Africanus recorded that in the sixteenth century, the town was ruled by a sultan of what he calls "Libyan" extraction. He noted a number of interesting facts about the town,

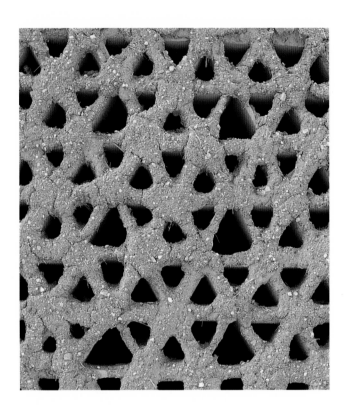

These triangular holes in a rosette pattern were designed to help air circulate in the attic.

Facing page: *The Baker's House is believed to have been built by a wealthy Libyan merchant in the nineteenth century. The reception room is richly sculpted.*

but made no mention of the famous Friday Mosque, known to the locals as *massalachibabba*, although he did note the existence of a similar mosque in Timbuktu. Only recently have researchers discovered the reason for this puzzling silence. In 1513, the year that Leo Africanus visited Agadez, the mosque had been standing for half a century, but work had not yet begun on the superb minaret, which stands roughly seventy feet (twenty-two meters) tall. The story goes that the minaret was built on the order of a holy man, Sheikh Zakarya, a native of Ghadamis, who had spent many years as a hermit, living in caves and forests, before the sultan discovered his existence and obliged him to come and live in the town. It is said that the minaret collapsed twice during the building works; in fact, traces of these ruins can still be seen. The legend of Sheikh Zakarya has it that the reason why the minaret collapsed twice was that the clay had not been paid for at an honest rate and that slave labor was being used. As the builders began work for the third time, Zakarya refused to countenance such dishonesty and profiteering, and he was finally able to complete the tower, a masterpiece of Islamic architecture. Like its counterpart in Timbuktu, the Agadez minaret—now an emblem for the whole of Niger—bristles with wooden stakes, giving rise to frequent comparisons to a hedgehog or a pincushion. This particular architectural feature has attracted a great deal of interest. The stakes are in fact part of the scaffolding used when the minaret was first built, and since they were left in place, they are still used whenever the structure undergoes renovation. The other major advantage of the wooden stakes is that they draw excess moisture out of the clay.

The sultan's palace lies just to the south of the great mosque. It is a vast building, designed for the sultan's retinue of some four hundred personal bodyguards and countless archers and horsemen, as well as the army, the sultan's family, staff, and the court—all long since vanished. It was here that the German explorer Heinrich Barth was granted an audience in the mid-nineteenth century, in a hall that he described in his travel journal as follows:

The rather low ceiling was supported by two short, stubby clay pillars, like wooden columns, slightly narrowing toward the ceiling, and each topped with a plain plank. On each plank a row of large planks were propped across the width of the room, and two similar rows across the length. These planks were holding up the roof, whose unevenly constructed inner frame could be seen. The frame of the roof was covered in a thick layer of branches tied down with matting. The whole structure was covered in a layer of compacted clay. Between the two pillars, at the far end of the hall, there was a heavy door leading to the inner rooms, while the side walls had two large openings for windows.

The architecture of the old part of the town reflects the origins of the traders who settled here. The town was once surrounded by a wall made of banco (clay mortar) measuring some three miles (five kilometers) in length. Since Agadez lies in an alluvial plain, clay has always been the most plentiful building material: the buildings, nearly all in the same shades of ocher beige, form a harmonious ensemble. The houses huddle together in blocks, separated by streets. In the narrowest passages, called *lak-lak*, the houses are so close together that there is just room for a person to slip between the walls. In the oldest houses, the floor is lower than the street, so that visitors step down into the rooms. This is because these houses were built on the very spot where the clay was extracted, so that less clay was

needed for the walls for the same floor surface. Later, the wealthier merchants began building houses with an upper floor. Certain elements in these buildings indicate a North African influence. The beams, for example, are made from palm trunks, and hollowed-out trunks are used to channel rainwater away from the vulnerable clay walls. The *tokotei* triangles that adorn each corner of the roof are sometimes shaped like pyramids, which has led some archaeologists to conjecture an Egyptian influence, although there is no other evidence to support this hypothesis. Over the doors are solid lintels made of palm trunks. The doorway is often framed by two *dakali*, benches built at the base of the walls to strengthen them. The window openings are few and far between, and generally small. Each window is decorated with raised geometric patterns made, like the other mural designs, of *kunku*, a mixture of clay and straw. Once inside the home, the visitor passes through two vestibules.

The first, called *shigifa*, was used to entertain visitors and guests, while the second, *shigifa-ta-biu*, led into the inner courtyard, *fili-n-guida*, which in turn led to the other rooms of the house, such as the kitchen (*foutei*) and bedrooms (*garubere*). The courtyard would also often have a ladder (*tchiktaren*) leading to the upper floor (*soro*).

The rooms were generally rather plain. The floor would be covered in mats. Objects were stored in niches in the thick walls, and clothes were piled on forked sticks. However, the houses that belonged to the wealthiest merchants, while rather ordinary-looking from the outside, were richly decorated on the inside. In the Baker's House, light plays on the geometric pattern of triangles and chevrons that adorns the walls, with here and there circles and rounded shapes breaking the rather rigid pattern. The overall effect is one of an organic, almost plant-like luxuriance.

The magnificently decorated interior of the Baker's House bears witness to the past splendors of Agadez, once a major trading center on the caravan routes, influenced by Tuareg, Arab, Hausa, Fulani, and Sudanese culture.

*A close-up view of the decoration in the Baker's House.
The raised and hollowed patterns are often picked out in
red and ornamented with geometric designs.*

Bernardo Bertolucci shot some scenes for his film The Sheltering Sky *in this room in the Baker's House.*

Following pages: *The façade of a typical Hausa home, with a terrace edged with an openwork balustrade.*

The triangular openings in the thick walls of a corridor in the Baker's House provide soft light and allow the air to circulate, while protecting the rooms from the heat of the day.

A house belonging to an Agadez merchant. The raised patterns around the doorway play with a combination of circles, semi-circles, triangles, and crescents.

These designs are characteristic of Hausa homes, which frequently feature raised patterns.

51

The motif of interlacing ovals is also found elsewhere
in Africa, for example, in Angola, where it is used
in rituals over the entrance to the fields where
circumcision is carried out or as a magical talisman
to ward off lion-men.

The "horns" atop these façades were probably designed with a protective function in mind. This is often the case for triangular or pointed shapes. Some homes have antelope antlers built into them, and truck drivers setting out across the desert often attach a pair to the radiator grill as a good luck charm.

The technique used to decorate traditional Hausa homes is halfway between sculpture and painting. The ocher banco is coated with a layer of clay into which vegetable matter has been kneaded. The patterns are then cut out of the clay. Today, some chemical pigments are used.

The use of industrial rather than natural pigments has opened up a whole range of new colors, used to their full advantage on this metal gate.

The techniques and materials may be modern, but the patterns remain traditional. The colors of this wrought iron motif soldered onto a metal gate are borrowed from the embroideries on the trousers worn by Tuareg men for centuries past.

The painted corrugated iron over this window (facing page) seems to borrow its hue from the heavy aquamarine veil worn by a modest young girl. The poet Arthur Rimbaud wrote: "I know it is Thou, who in this place, Minglest thine almost Saharan blue!"

In the Sahara, sand can be used to explain a route, draw the course of a wadi, teach the ancient tifinagh writing still used by the Tuaregs, or to trace patterns and designs before they are transferred to the walls of a new building.

Facing page: This magnificent antelope was sculpted directly on the wall of a house in Agadez. The wavy lines of the backdrop represent rolling sand dunes.

THE STONE HOUSES
OF MAURITANIA

Mauritania is a large country, measuring 398,000 square miles (1,030,700 square km), just 0.48 percent of which is arable, to support a population of nearly three million. Mauritania has a uniquely rich heritage. It boasts a fabulous wealth of prehistoric settlements and magnificent oases in the style known as Saharan Berber.

Some four thousand years ago, a group of Neolithic herders chose to settle on the slopes of an isolated rocky escarpment, lying between two oceans of sand, the Majabat al-Kubra in the north and the Aouker dunes in the south. It is likely that they had traveled down from the north, forced to leave their home region because of the encroaching sands of the Sahara. They settled by the only cliff in the whole region, towering one hundred and eighty feet (sixty meters) over the Aouker dunes in places, which promised sites that were easy to defend from attack, and—even more importantly—the only lakes in the region that had survived the creeping desertification, and the fresh pasture where they could graze their animals. The escarpment where these early inhabitants settled is known today as Dhar Tichit. It prolongs the curve of Dhar Ou Senn, which, together with the eastern flanks Dhar Oualata and Dhar Nema, forms a semi-circle stretching five hundred miles (800 km) between the Tagant and Nema, a town some hundred miles (150 km) to the north of the border with Mali. Along the curve lie the towns of Boumdeid, Akreijit, Tichit, and Oualata. *Dhar* is an Arabic term meaning plateau, but in these place names, it refers to the cliff itself.

The earliest inhabitants soon discovered that the region was blessed with an exceptional microclimate, thanks to the seasonal rains that swept up from the Gulf of Guinea. The climate was sufficiently wet to grow nettle trees, which require a minimum annual rainfall of eighteen inches (forty-five centimeters). The land was typical savanna, dotted with trees. Elephants, rhinoceros, crocodiles, and hippopotamus were common. Their bones can be seen scattered around the long, dry watering holes and in the sand, which also hides the fossilized roots of reed beds. Other species, such as giraffes, antelopes, and ostriches, that

A close-up view of a wall. Triangles of blue schist found in the region of Tichit, Mauritania, have been built into the wall to form one large triangle.

Facing page: *The street leading to the Tichit mosque. The doorway to the mosque itself is ornamented with a recess in the form of a triangular pediment with stepped, corbeled edges.*

Preceding pages: *The rectangular blocks of stone used to build houses in Tichit are all nearly the same size, giving an overall impression of harmony and stability.*

did not need such abundant water supplies, survived in the region for longer, but eventually became extinct in their turn. The ostrich population died out in the last century.

To the east of Tichit is the village of Akreijit, which dates back to protohistoric times (roughly 3000–1000 B.C.E.). The walls of the houses are in dry stone and built without mortar. In 1934, the great explorer and naturalist Théodore Monod carried out the first scientific study of a Saharan prehistoric village here. Since then, archaeologists have affectionately called the village Monodville. Today, the village, on an outcrop over a dried-up lakebed, consists of approximately 180 enclosures, all huddled together, as in more modern Saharan villages. The site covers an area of some eight acres (twenty hectares), and is surrounded by a solid defensive wall. Below the village, grain was stored in shelters protected by overhanging rocks along the cliff face. There is plenty of evidence that the village was a busy, thriving place from around 1500 B.C.E. for a thousand years or more. The herdsmen tended their flocks at the foot of the cliff, making stone tools as they watched the animals grazing. The animals were vitally important to the community, and may even have played a specifically symbolic role—terra-cotta statuettes and cave paintings of sheep and cattle have been found at the site. The largest painting is of a cow, and measures over twelve feet (four meters) in length. It is in a narrow natural corridor in the rock that lies on an east-west axis above the Akreijit cliff. The site is so exceptional that it is hard not to believe that some sort of religious feeling at least partially inspired the painting.

Archaeologists have recorded a total of nearly four hundred prehistoric settlements in the Dhar Tichit region. They ranged in population from maybe a dozen dwellings to a quite sizable town of six hundred or so buildings at Dakhlet el-Atrouss, which would have been home to one thousand to three thousand people. Some of the settlements were fairly loosely knit, but others were already developing a real town structure. The quality of the protohistoric architecture in the region can be judged by the number of walls still standing, ranging in height from twenty inches to six feet (fifty centimeters to two meters). Visitors must use their imagination to see the houses as they were, with wooden beams and door lintels, thatched roofs, inner walls, a coating of banco on the outer walls, and decorative touches of wicker, wood, and leather. The enclosures, similar to those found in many parts of Africa to this day, are roughly round, triangular, or rectangular in shape. They often contain two or three rows of monolithic pillars with three pillars in each line; it has been suggested that they were once the bases of millet storerooms. The walls are up to three feet (one meter) thick in some parts, and are inset with storage niches and doors with paved thresholds. The villages were laid out around public spaces like modern town squares. The larger towns, which were home to tens of thousands of people, even had recognizably modern streets. Inhabited zones have also been discovered elsewhere on the plateau, in a geological depression or *baten* (stomach in Arabic) at the foot of the cliff, and in the Tagant region.

Some of the inhabitants would go fishing on the lake with spears and nets, to catch silurid fish or Nile perch. Others went hunting armed with bows and arrows. The women would gather large snails to eat, and grind pearl millet into coarse flour with sandstone millstones. Archaeologists working in the Dhar Tichit region have uncovered fragments of pottery where millet seeds became embedded in the still moist clay. In the oldest pottery shards, the millet was from a wild species, while in more recent fragments, the grain was

A *wall of squared stones with an earth mortar, partially protected by a coating of clay. Akreijit, Mauritania.*

Preceding pages: *View of Tichit and its palm garden, dominated by cliffs. In the foreground is a* tikkit, *or hut, made of palm leaves and stalks.*

from farmed varieties. Thanks to this combination of natural resources—hunting, fishing, herding, and farming—the local population flourished, before slipping into a gradual decline as the climate grew hotter and drier. By 500 B.C.E., the climate in the region reached the extreme conditions that prevail to this day. The first inhabitants of Monodville could no longer hope to survive in such an inhospitable environment. As the lakes dried up, it became ever harder to sustain the ancestral lifestyle. The population steadily declined until the last inhabitants of the region headed south and west in search of fresh pastures, as their ancestors had done centuries before. The region was empty until the introduction of horses and later dromedaries, when nomads once more began to roam the open spaces. They in their turn left cave paintings of men riding horses or camels hunting addax (a species of antelope) and ostriches. The villages of Dhar Tichit had long since been abandoned and the last few oxbow lakes dried up when these paleo-Berber peoples arrived in the region c. 500 B.C.E. For centuries, the villages were seen by the people of Tichit and Akreijit as a useful source of millstones and pestles, left behind by the original inhabitants.

In the past, archaeologists looking for evidence of the types of early urbanization found around the Mediterranean and in the Middle East jumped to the rather hasty conclusion that there were no signs of comparable architectural planning in Africa. Consequently, they claimed that the Great Zimbabwe ruins could only have been the work of non-native populations. They even argued that the highly unusual chain of settlements at Dhar Tichit—the only one of its kind in all of Africa—could not be termed an urban civilization, despite the fact that it

represented a coherent architectural style over a period of more than a thousand years and a distance of some two hundred and fifty miles (four hundred km), stretching from one end of the semi-circle of the *dhar* to the other. However archaeologists have now come to acknowledge that the ensemble of settlements represents a perfectly valid vision of architecture and urban planning unique to Africa. The long, low constructions—built where possible avoiding the use of straight lines, organized in juxtaposed or huddled clusters with public spaces between each group of dwellings—were uniquely suited to the expectations of the local community.

After climate change had forced most of the inhabitants of the Dhar Tichit region to migrate, it is likely that some of them ended up in what is now Ghana, where there is evidence that they played a role in the foundation of the great towns of the ancient Ghanaian empire by the eighth century. The town we know as Tegdaoust is none other than the ancient city of Audaghost, founded in the eighth century. The ruins of the Muslim city spread over several square miles and to a depth of several meters. They were built on the ruins of ancient pre-Islamic buildings. Archeological digs have demonstrated that by the tenth century, the floor plans of these Islamic-style rectangular houses were very similar to the homes in the modern oasis town of Oualata. Visitors would enter the home through a door giving directly onto the street, stepping into the first of two courtyards. The bedrooms lay off the courtyards, and were much smaller than the yards themselves. It is thought that the capital of this ancient Ghanaian empire was the town of Koumbi Saleh, one hundred and twenty five miles (two hundred km) southwest of Oualata and some twenty-five miles (forty km) to the north of the modern

The walls of Akreijit look as if they are built of dry stone, as the clay mortar, or banco, has long since vanished.

A decorative recess on the façade of the Tichit mosque, surrounded by triangular motifs formed of rough-hewn tiles of schist.

border with Mali. It is an extraordinarily rich archeological site, with several square miles of ancient ruins built in schist, to a depth of more than twenty feet (seven meters).

Only with the introduction of the dromedary to the Dhar Tichit-Oualata region some time after the first century C.E. were men able to travel in the Sahara again. They rediscovered the ancient routes across the desert, stopping at the watering holes that were few and far between. Thanks to the astounding capacity of the camel to go forty or even fifty days without drinking, the southern regions of Mauritania, the Tagant plateau and the Hodh Depression, stranded between two endless expanses of desert, were no longer completely isolated, and could even be said to have enjoyed something of a renaissance.

Tichit, the former capital of the Tagant region, and Oualata, the main town in the Hodh region, both lie on one of the oldest trans-Saharan routes, linking the Mediterranean coast and the Sudan—a term meaning the black country used by the Arabs to refer to all of sub-Saharan Africa, not just the modern state of Sudan. The route also led to Timbuktu and Gao via the Taghaza or Tatantal salt mines, described by the Andalusian geographer al-Bakri in 1068: "Among the extraordinary things in this desert is a salt mine, two day's walk from al-Majabat al-Kubra (the great desert), twenty stages from Sijilmassa. The ground is excavated as when mining for metals or precious gemstones. At a depth of less than two toises [twelve feet], the miners find the salt, which they extract like stone in a quarry. This mine is called Tatantal. Over it stands a castle whose walls, halls, crenels, and turrets are built of blocks of salt." This last detail echoes a passage from Herodotus, writing in the fifth century B.C.E., which states that in the regions to the west of the Libyan desert "are a salt mine and local inhabitants. The homes of all these men are built with blocks of salt." The salt mined in the Sahara was exchanged for gold and ivory, but the trading routes were also used for transporting slaves. In 1790, the French artist Venture de Paradis wrote of this abominable trade in his *Notes sur l'Atlas et le Sahara*, "Negroes are bought for tablets of salt an inch thick or for a belt worth ten to twelve francs. Many of these Sudanese [i.e. sub-Saharan Africans], who are not used to suffering thirst, die on the route across the Sahara; but the price at which the survivors are sold on the Barbary Coast is high enough to make it a lucrative trade." The scholar al-Amin el-Chenguitti wrote in 1913: "Everything in Sudan [sub-Saharan Africa] can be bought with salt: horses, bolts of cloth, millet, and slaves." He continued that he had heard stories that some parents sold off their children in exchange for salt, and added that slaves were sold "according to the size of their feet." Once they had reached the trading towns beyond the southern fringes of the desert, the traders unloaded their blocks of salt. They measured the feet of the slaves they wished to buy, and cut a corresponding length off the block of salt to give to the slave trader. A certain Augustin Bernard, writing in the then French colony of Algeria in the 1930s, noted that locals referred to blacks as *gemt el-melah*, or shackles of salt, "because formerly they were sold in Sudan in exchange for a block of salt."

Wealthy merchants settled in the southern Sahara, where caravans had long joined forces before setting out on the seven-hundred-mile (1000-km) journey across the desert, taking goods to sell in the towns along the route—Qasr el-Barka, el-Rachid, Tidjikdja, Tichit, and Akreijit. This route was also regularly used by pilgrims on their way to Mecca or to Oualata, the easternmost town on the desert crossing. Oualata lay at the crossroads of this route from east to west and another route that led to Kayes on the River Senegal, passing through Timbedra and Nioro.

Over time, doubtless due to its position at the crossroads of these two major routes, the town of Oualata became an important center of Islamic culture. Of course, it should be noted that in this context, the term "route" does not refer to an actual road, but rather to a fixed itinerary across the vast emptiness of the desert. Tichit lies some one hundred and ninety miles (300 km) from Oualata; wells such as the one at Aratane, lying on the frontier between the Hodh and Tagant regions, were all that stood between the travelers and a slow and painful death by thirst.

At the height of the trans-Saharan trade, from the fourteenth to the seventeenth centuries, caravans of several hundred camels, each carrying a burden of four blocks of salt weighing a total of between 220 and 350 pounds (100 to 160 kg), would set out for a journey lasting a month from Ouadane to Oualata, with another fifteen days to reach Timbuktu.

In the eighteenth century, the salt mines of Taghaza were abandoned, and the trading oases entered a period of gradual decline as trade centered on Timbuktu, the final destination of a new caravan route from Touat via Taoudeni, a famous salt mine in the north of what is now Mali. At the same time a series of blows were dealt to trans-Saharan trade: salt was massively imported from Europe, dates were no longer a staple foodstuff, the ivory

The entrance to the Tichit mosque. Above the doorway is a recess. Each step of the pediment is decorated with a slab of schist, each in a different color, forming a triangle. The tympanum is likewise decorated with triangle shapes.

A house in Tichit surrounded by heaps of salt.

trade was prohibited, and the demand for ostrich plumes collapsed. The final nail in the coffin of the oases was the growth of the anti-slavery movement across Europe in the nineteenth century. Slavery was abolished in Denmark in 1803, Britain in 1834, and France in 1848. In the 1870s, sea salt shipped to the west coast of Africa, to ports all along the Gulf of Guinea, was three times less expensive than salt mined in the Sahara. By the 1950s, the cost of salt in the Sahara had risen to ten times the price along the coast. As a consequence, salt mined in the Sahara was a costly luxury, to be used only for ritual or medical purposes. The collapse of the Saharan economy inevitably led to the decline of the oases. As the eminent specialist in African history Raymond Mauny noted, "The towns of the Sahara were born of trade, and the departure of the traders has condemned them to death."

Let us follow one of the caravans across the Sahara in the days when trade was still flourishing. We will take the *tariq el-Lemtuni*, or eastern route, from Sijilmassa to the Lemtuna region in the south of Mauritania and onto the town of Timbuktu, in modern-day Mali. Our route will take us through the oasis towns of Ouadane, Chinguetti, Tichit, and Oualata.

Our journey begins in Ouadane. According to local tradition, the town was founded in either 1147 or 1329. Like all of the towns along the northern fringe of the Sahel, Ouadane owed its wealth to trade. In the fifteenth century, it was visited by the Venetian navigator Alvise da Cà da Mosto, who was in the service of the Portuguese court. He noted that silks from Granada and Tunis were on sale in exchange for gold. He also noted,

"in these sandy places, lions, leopards, and ostriches abound." In its heyday, Ouadane had as many as three thousand houses; nowadays, only four hundred remain, and the population has fallen to under a thousand. The building materials are the same as those used further south—blocks of stone, conveniently split into slabs and rubble by the searing heat, are plentiful in the region. The stone walls were built using banco, a type of clay mortar, although this has generally been worn away by wind erosion; in fact, at first glance, the walls seem to be built of dry stone. While it is certainly the case that even in prosperous times, some dwellings had to be abandoned for various reasons, visitors to the town today are left with the impression that the desert is gradually reclaiming its due, and that in a few decades, there will be nothing here but baking sands. A local proverb says that Ouadane lies on the confluent of the Wadi of Knowledge and the Wadi of Palm Trees, meaning that the town owes its existence to wisdom and to wealth. However, fortune has not smiled on the town for many years. The old mosque, in the southwestern part of the town, may have been a witness of Ouadane's past splendors. Its date of construction is far from certain, although it is believed to have been built in the twelfth century and abandoned in the mid-fifteenth century. Inside the mosque are some fine Moorish arches—a style found nowhere else in this region—which might suggest an unsuccessful attempt by an architect visiting from the north to import a new building technique. The site of the former minaret, which collapsed long ago, is marked by a pile of stones. The new mosque has a tall, square minaret

The ancient town of Chinguetti in Mauritania is dominated by the minaret of the mosque, which rises to a height of some thirty feet (ten meters). It has a square base, and each corner of the structure is topped with a spike bearing an ostrich egg, a symbol of hope.

that doubles as a watchtower. It looms over the old *ksar* that seems to while away the centuries in patient slumber at the foot of the mountain.

Roughly sixty-five miles (one hundred kilometers) to the south of Ouadane is the ancient town of Chinguetti. The town can be seen from a distance, thanks to a thirty-foot (ten-meter) minaret similar to the one in Ouadane. A flight of twenty steps leads to the top of the tower, where there is a terrace protected by a wall. At each corner of the tower is a stick holding aloft an ostrich egg (a symbol of hope). Medieval bestiaries recounted how ostriches left their eggs buried in the sand. The bird thus became a symbol for the humility and abnegation of the saints who left their families to seek God in the desert—*eremo* in Greek, hence the term "hermit." There is archaeological evidence of the use of ostrich eggs in religious rituals in the Sahara dating back to at least protohistory; for example, many have been found buried in tumuli. Copts in southern Ethiopia place ostrich eggs on the tombs of their dead, and Coptic Orthodox churches have the eggs hanging from the vault to represent steadfast watchfulness. Ostrich eggs are also found in places of worship in the Arab world, where they were decorated with leather straps, inscribed with calligraphy, and hung from mosque lamps in honor of the caliph. The eggs are emblematic of hope and fertility, and their perfectly smooth curves are a symbol of perfection and imagination. The eggs atop the minaret thus play an important symbolic role, noted as early as the thirteenth century by a Norman troubadour, Guillaume le Clerc, in a text entitled *Le Bestiaire Divin* (The Divine Bestiary): "Icest oisel nos senefie / le prodrome de bone vie / Qui let les choses terriennes / Et se prend à célestiennes" (This bird indicates the start of the righteous life, leaving behind earthly concerns to devote itself to celestial ones). In time, Chinguetti became a major religious center, one of the seven holy places of Islam, where pilgrims would gather before setting out for Mecca. Its economic and cultural domination was such that the whole country was known as Bilad or Trab Chinguiti (the land of Chinguetti) before being renamed Mauritania in 1904 (the name was taken from the ancient Roman name for the province, Mauretania Tingitana).

The biographies of the great Chinguetti scholars tell how they were schooled in the town, which was highly unusual and in itself an indication of Chinguetti's cultural importance. It was more usual for scholars to study far from home, in accordance with the Prophet's Hadith: "Seek knowledge, even as far as China!" From the eighteenth century to the early twentieth century, Chinguetti attracted many scholars, who traveled huge distances to study with the great masters in the holy town. Some of these scholars took the title *el-Chingiti* to indicate that they had studied there and as a mark of respectability. The inhabitants of Chinguetti considered it an honor to house and feed the visiting scholars, and even copied manuscripts for them. Given such a rich intellectual heritage, it is no great surprise to discover that today, a higher proportion of girls attend school in Chinguetti than anywhere else in the country.

Our journey now takes us to the Tagant region and the town of Tidjikdja before we come to the Hodh region. The style of buildings here is typical of Saharan architecture in general. The houses have just a few small square openings in the walls to protect the interiors from the crushing heat and blinding sunlight. The streets are narrow, providing shade, and turn at sharp angles to allow passers-by to escape from the wind and stinging sand. The terraces are ringed with battlements, while the corners of the roofs are topped with triangles to protect against demons that become entangled in them. Inside the homes, the floors are of beaten

The blue shutters of this house complement the delicate pastel tones of the schist.

earth. Objects are stored in niches in the thick walls coated with a layer of clay. The base of the walls is often strengthened by built-in benches. The homes are built with one overriding need in mind: to protect the inhabitants from the heat of the day. Other architectural elements, however, give the buildings a more distinct local character. In the west of the Tagant region, in Qasr el-Barka, each house has one or two inner courtyards strewn with sand, with a single door leading into the home. The façades are adorned with stones arranged in herringbone patterns, or in rows of triangles forming a zigzag separated by horizontally placed blocks of stone. The lintels above the doors are made of a slab of stone or a beam of wood. The doors, or *fumm* (from the Arabic term for a mouth or opening), are generally made of *talha*, or acacia wood. Visitors entering the house must step over a board to keep sand out.

In the east of the Tagant region, in Tichit, the central part of a traditional home generally consists of a room giving onto an inner courtyard and leading into the storeroom and attic. Here the preferred style of decoration consists of patterns of long slabs of green schist. The same slabs are used for the thresholds, lintels, and sometimes corbels. The lintels are often framed by stepped pediments to reduce the weight on the stone slab. In smaller buildings, the superb triangular pediment is often broken down into a series of smaller triangles

The dark horizontal stripes on this young woman's wrap seem to echo the bands of stone typical of the local architecture.

A haphazard coating round the windows, slightly asymmetrical lines, and drips of bold blue paint: this façade in Chinguetti may not look tidy, but it is certainly dynamic.

arranged in a chevron pattern. Some doors display a particular technical innovation: the lintel rests on two hewn corbels, which in turn rest on a small slab that extends beyond the door frame. This means that a shorter lintel beam can be used without having a narrower doorway.

This technique was also in use in the ancient town of Koumbi Saleh, while the open triangles are also found in the equally ancient town of Audaghost. Théodore Monod tried to establish a link between the honeycombed decoration typical of Tichit architecture and a similar style found in the ruins of Great Zimbabwe thousands of miles away, in southern Africa. However, such a link is far from conclusive, since other examples of a similar style have been found in Angola and Portugal. The shared use of such motifs does not furnish sufficient evidence to trace the pattern of cultural influence, since similar designs are used all over the world, wherever the principal building material is square blocks of stone or brick. Two motifs in particular lend themselves to stone or brick walls: a herringbone pattern, which the Romans called *opus spicatum* (literally, spiked work) and which is found on many European churches, and rows of aligned or superposed triangles. This second motif is so basic that it is hardly surprising that it was discovered independently in a number of different cultures. Given the nature of the materials and the very basic patterns used, it is entirely feasible that the builders of Tichit came up with the decorative motifs of their own accord. There is really no evidence that the herringbone, diamond, zigzag, and chevron

patterns built into the walls of Tichit were influenced by similar designs at the top of the walls around the oasis gardens in the Fezzan region, or by the clay brick designs found in the Senufo culture of the Ivory Coast, or the stone patterns of the Great Zimbabwe ruins.

Archaeologists have seen a common influence in the slabs of green schist built as decoration into the walls of houses in Tichit, and examples in medieval Bantu architecture. However, it has been shown that the same technique was widely used in the Mediterranean basin and the Levant. It therefore seems likely that this was again a case of builders independently coming up with the same solution to technical difficulties. The adventurer Odette de Puigaudeau pointed out that using such slabs is a way of getting over the problem of uneven floors. The Tichit mosque is thought to date from the fourteenth century. It has a square minaret standing fifty feet (sixteen meters) high, separate from the main body of the mosque. It was built in 1842 as a copy of the former minaret. Tichit owes its existence to the trade between Ouadane and Oualata, but it soon became a major halt for caravans transporting salt from Idjil. As early as the thirteenth century, much of Tichit's wealth came from plantations of twenty thousand palm trees; this had once been a region of lakes and the water table remained very close to the surface. In the mid-nineteenth century, Tichit was home to a population of three thousand. Today, there are barely a thousand inhabitants, and the desert sands threaten to engulf the almost empty streets entirely.

A Mauritanian woman walking along a street in Tichit almost choked with sand.

Close-up views of stone and schist decorative motifs on the façade of a house in Chinguetti.

Following pages:
Left: *In Tichit, the doors are generally ornamented with nails with decorative metal heads.* Right: *On this door in a home in Chinguetti, the old wooden bolt, patterned with delicate carvings, is now merely decorative; the owner has installed a brand new metal bolt.*

THE STONE HOUSES OF MAURITANIA·85
footer here

These double doors
are closed by a large
wooden bolt.

Facing page: *Façade of
a house in Chinguetti.*

The Chinguetti mosque.

Facing page: *It is hard to tell whether this pattern in a Chinguetti home stands out from the wall or is hollowed into it until the shadows in the triangles and at the base of the metal object give it away.*

*The façade of a recent house in Chinguetti,
built with a combination of modern techniques
and traditional decorations.*

The inner courtyard of the Habott family home in Chinguetti. The home was acquired by the Mauritanian government to house a library grouping the town's manuscripts. The walls are decorated with irregularly spaced triangular and square niches.

A square pillar inset with triangular niches in Mohamed Ould Ghoulam's home in Chinguetti. At the base of the pillar stands a tablet inscribed with verses of the Koran, once used for teaching in a Koranic school.

The main room in the Habott family home. Generally, the size of the room depends on the length of the tree trunks available for use as beams. Here, this constraint has been overcome by the use of pillars to support the ceiling.

The main room in the Habott family home, which will soon be used as a library.

THE RED WALLS OF OUALATA

Our journey now brings us to the last major halt before Timbuktu, which is now some three hundred and fifty miles (five hundred kilometers) distant. In the heart of the Hodh desert, the red walls of the *ksar* of Oualata stand on a cliff, dominating the dry, dusty landscape. The buildings are in a rather austere style. In the fourteenth century, Oualata was the empire of Mali's earliest customs post. The town enjoyed its greatest wealth in the sixteenth century. The streets are narrow, and twist and turn between the houses. A typical home in Oualata has walls coated with a protective layer of banco, an upper floor, and benches at the foot of the outer walls to strengthen them at the base. These benches are particularly appreciated by the town's elders for resting and chatting with friends.

The doors giving onto the street are often studded with patterns of nails with decorative metal heads, and framed with plain moldings. The door leads into an inner hall, where many families have put up a tent structure. A degree of privacy is assured by the large wooden bolts on the doors, which can be locked from the outside using a wooden key. On either side of the door is a series of pillars which strengthen the walls, but which are also rather decorative. There are two or three steps up to the front door to stop sand. The frame of the roof is generally made of palm trunks split lengthwise. The trunks are laid in place with the flat side facing up so that the exposed sapwood can absorb water from the roof and the bark is exposed to the hot air that rises up from the rooms below. The flat side of the trunks swells as it absorbs the water, and the bark contracts in the hot air. The beam takes on a convex form, a good strong shape to support the weight of the hollow blocks. This traditional method for strengthening a roof structure was described by the geographer Strabo in the first century B.C.E. The builders of Oualata also discovered another technique to strengthen their roofs: they use long beams that protrude beyond the outer walls, drawing off excess moisture that

Rosette motifs, frequently found on the walls of Oualata,
Mauritania, have been the cause of much debate.
It is not clear whether they are simply intricate
geometrical forms, or whether they have a more profound
symbolic resonance whose secret has been lost.

evaporates in the breeze. Such details prove that Saharan architecture is far from being primitive, as was long claimed; on the contrary, the design of these homes is extremely well adapted to the local climate, and makes best use of the available building materials. This explains why attempts to modernize the local architectural style were generally doomed to failure, since they did not take these factors into account. Odette de Puigaudeau, writing in 1960, gives a typical example: "In constructions built by the Europeans, the beams always give at the ends because the architects reject indigenous techniques out of hand, and enclose the ends of the beams within the walls. They quickly rot, because the timber used is too green. The Europeans then say that date-palm wood is not resistant enough, and prefer to use stretches of train rails. Apart from the fact that these thin metal girders look weak and inelegant, they buckle, so that the hollow blocks sag and a damp patch grows in the center of the ceiling, so that the girders there rust and break in just a few years."

The typical home is similar to houses in the Tagant region, with two important differences: the walls are coated in a layer of clay, and the openings in the inner walls—windows, niches, and doors—are framed with magnificent white and ocher patterns. These are either in the form of geometric designs in bas-relief, where the white stands out boldly against the red walls, or red lines painted against a white background. The two are often used together to create extravagant, highly symbolic motifs. Each door has a small niche, decorated the same way, set into the wall on either side. Inside the homes, the ornamentation is often exuberant, with patterns carved into the clay coating on the wall. The motifs are given a layer of whitewash. The women then pick out the lines of the carved pattern with a finger dipped in a dark red pigment. Since the 1950s, the palette of colors has expanded with the introduction of chemical paints, so that alongside the traditional reds and ochers, some houses now boast superb compositions in indigo, yellow, and green, although the window frames are always left white.

Similar painted motifs are to be found elsewhere in sub-Saharan Africa, for example in northern Nigeria and in Ghadamis. In each case, the patterns are the work of women. The colors gradually fade or are worn away through exposure to the elements, and need to be touched up regularly. The women do this once a year, in the autumn, at the end of the rainy season. They begin by giving the part of the wall to be decorated a fresh coat of whitewash. They then pick out the patterns again, following the carved lines with a finger dipped in a mixture which is traditionally made of brown ocher, charcoal, cow dung, and crushed gum arabic mixed with water. Specialists have long debated the origins and symbolism of these patterns. It was thought that the white frames around the doors might have been inspired by the interlacing patterns painted in red on a white background that were common in twelfth-century Islamic art from Marrakech. The rosette patterns placed above the doors and round the ablution stones were thought to have been influenced by the four-foiled rosette motifs on paneling from the Almoravid dynasty (c. 1056–1147), also in Marrakech.

Together with her fellow traveler Marion Sénones, the explorer Odette de Puigaudeau published detailed reproductions of a number of the decorative motifs after a visit to Oualata in 1937. However, in the accompanying text, she wrote that "the explanation [for the patterns] had to be sought a long way from Oualata, in other countries and other times, in the treasures of libraries." She devoted a great deal of time to reading articles on prehistory, trying to find possible influences for the Oualata paintings, even suggesting at one point

that they might be inspired by examples of Mesolithic art in Mas-d'Azil, in southwestern France. She also took as evidence comparable designs in Morocco, Tunisia, Egypt, and Spain, which may well be possible influences given the importance of trans-Saharan trade. However, it seems extremely far-fetched to see a possible link, as she does, between the Oualata designs and similar motifs recorded as far afield as Yugoslavia, Persia, the Indus valley, the Marquesas Islands in the South Pacific, and Easter Island.

Given that similar designs have been found all over the world, it seems more logical to ask whether research has not hitherto relied on overly generalized descriptions to try and find common elements, or whether the designs themselves are in fact so basic that they could easily have arisen independently in different traditions. The rule is to bear in mind that the more basic the graphic elements, the less likely they are to correspond to a particular style. Conversely, the more complex the pattern, the more significant it is to find it used in different places. To take a straightforward example, there is only one way to draw a circle and very few ways to draw a spiral. Therefore, the fact that circles and spirals have

The inner courtyard is both a place of rest and the center of the home; it leads to the granary, the attic, the bedrooms, and to the other rooms in the house.

Preceding pages: *The ocher walls of this inner courtyard in Oualata are decorated with the magnificent motifs for which the town is justly famous.*

The "ears" on either side of this doorway are a variation on the traditional niches, or muchemma, *generally built into the wall. The niches contain an ablution stone in dark, shiny schist, which has come to take the place of the Ka'aba, the sacred stone in Mecca. Visitors must purify themselves by touching the stone before they enter the home.*

been found in traditional art in various parts of the world cannot be considered significant in terms of influence: they appear in everything from cave paintings to architecture and modern abstract art. It would be ridiculous to see this as evidence for transcontinental cultural influence. Yet this is the trap that Odette de Puigaudeau fell into in her research into the Oualata mural decoration. She set out to look for specific design elements, such as patterns derived from the Arabic letter *waw*, resembling a comma, which feature heavily in the Oualata motifs. Of course, by taking ornamental elements out of context, she was able to find similar patterns on Moorish harps, Syrian trays, and Senegalese and Sudanese embroideries. But this cannot be taken as proof of influence.

It is pointless to try to extrapolate a meaning from "other countries and other times, in the treasures of libraries"—a meaning that might be wholly inappropriate to the context in question. The best—indeed the only—way to make sense of such a richly symbolic system is to look at the society that created it, and the role it plays within that society. This was the approach taken in 1948 and 1949 by G. J. Duchemin. He interviewed the wives of two

builders, who worked on mural patterns. The women proved a rich source of information. Duchemin's findings were later developed by Jean Gabus. Thanks to these two men, we now know that Oualata's traditional decorative patterns are based on a series of basic motifs called either *al-tarha al-kabira* (large motifs) or *al-tarha al-sghira* (small motifs). The niches on either side of the doors are called *muchemma* (lamp) and contain an ablution stone in polished schist called *tayammum*. Before entering, visitors must touch the stone to purify themselves. The friezes around the doors are called *turraha*, as is the chain that shuts the door inside. The friezes thus symbolically reinforce the protection of the home. Other motifs are a four-leaf-clover shape called *al-kitab* (the book), which serves as an amulet, and a mushroom shape that represents *udhen gorg*, or the tag on the heel of a woman's *babouche* (leather slipper). Another series of motifs, placed in complex patterns above the doors, represented stylized human figures, including *aroudgij*, or people—in fact men; *azba*, the virgin; *mra's-ghira*, the young woman; *msulfa*, the woman with long tresses, in her thirties; *mra'kebira*, the matron; and on top *umm lehraïgfat*, or the mother with hips, a powerful fertility symbol.

The benches built on either side of the door serve a dual role: they provide a resting place for weary passers-by, and strengthen the walls of the home.

Preceding pages: *Oualata as seen from the cliff that stands over the town.*

The women are responsible for decorating their homes. The rosettes in the courtyards are often topped with a symbol of female fertility called Umm lehraïgfat or "mother with hips."

Each element of the Oualata murals has a name evocative of a rich symbolism of womanhood: azba *(the virgin),* tfaila *(the young girl),* mra'sghira *(the young woman),* mra'kebira *(the matron), and* msulfa *(the woman with long tresses).*

Facing page: A woman playing sig, *a variation on a game found throughout Africa that only women are allowed to play.*

It is unlikely that further research will change our interpretation of these mural decorations. However, the information that we do have is quite sufficient to give us a fascinating glimpse into the symbols and rituals of this society. Much of the mural decoration is found around doorways, indicating an important symbolic role for the notion of the passage. It is hardly surprising to find amulets, ablution stones, and symbolic chains around the doors. Thresholds are seen as having magical properties in many societies all over the world. On the other hand, it is most unusual, particularly in an Islamic society, to find passages placed under the protection of the "mother with hips," a female figure with legs spread wide, dominating all the others. Entering a room through a doorway decorated with this motif is a potent image of the return to the womb, a powerfully resonant ritual concept in much of sub-Saharan Africa, as André Mary has demonstrated. Crossing a threshold decorated with a mother figure in a ritual representation of the act of giving birth may well itself be a symbolic reversal of the birthing process, a return to the mother's uterus. The home is a symbolic representation of the mother's body; by renewing the mural decorations annually, the women are in fact heralding the rebirth of their society.

The vertical patterns on the walls here include the "little man" motif—two semi-circles back to back—and the kitab, or amulet motif of four semi-circles forming a cross with curved arms.

The stairway leading up to the terrace is framed by a stepped pattern on the wall. The stairs themselves are ornamented with squares on each step, giving the impression of a carpet running down to the bottom.

The wall is coated with red ocher and a layer of sand and lime. The women of the house have just finished repainting the motifs partly worn away through exposure to the elements.

The Oualata library. The motifs were long believed to be calligraphic symbols, but it has recently been shown that this is not the case. The turraha, or chains framing the square niches in the pillar, are also to be found around the main doorways of houses throughout the town.

This style of rosette, often found in the center of
decorative motifs, is traditionally held to represent
four young women or girls.

Above and preceding pages: *The women dip their index finger into a mix of red, yellow, or brown pigments and trace patterns on the freshly whitewashed walls, following the lines of the motif carved into the wall. The pigments traditionally used are brown ocher, charcoal, cow dung, and crushed gum arabic extracted from acacia trees, mixed with water.*

The inner courtyard of a house and the stairs
leading up to the terrace. Here, the motifs
have not been renewed for a long while,
although their outline is still visible. Above
the lintel of the door, the "mother with hips"
can be clearly distinguished over a group of
young girls. The door itself is framed
with a chain pattern.

The inner courtyard of a house where all the openings have been framed in white.

Both the Bible and the Koran were born in nomadic cultures. Archaeologists have found evidence of ancient Mesopotamian shepherds sacrificing sheep and goats to win the favor of the gods—a tradition that continues in many nomadic cultures to this day.

Facing page: An elderly Mauritanian man, dressed in a boubou, standing in front of his house. The door is decorated with ornamental nail heads, metal strips, and an impressive doorknocker.

124

Front doors are often decorated with two muchemma'
medallions.

Facing page: *Above this doorway is the symbol of the*
msulfa, *the woman with long braids. The squares and
diamond shapes ornamented with crosses are stylized
amulets, there to protect the home and its inhabitants.*

Another doorway framed by a chain pattern and with a msulfa *above the door. On either side is the symbol called* aroudgij *(people). The medallion round the* muchemma' *uses a broader range of colors than is traditional, including blue and yellow, more commonly found on pottery.*

The square at the center of the muchemma' *medallion symbolizes the black Ka'aba stone; the wavy lines represent pilgrims in Mecca.*

On either side of the doorway, a stepping stone places the ablution stone—here, set in a multicolored design— within easy reach.

A *multicolored* muchemma' *medallion.*

*Illuminations in an Arabic manuscript
in the Oualata library.*

Multicolored designs around the doorway to a house.
The yellow S shapes (facing page) are thought to
represent the Arabic letter **waw**—the only male
element in the overwhelmingly female symbolism in
traditional Oualata house decoration.

A view of Oualata. In the foreground is the mosque. It is a relatively recent construction, built to replace the old mosque, destroyed by a tornado on August 22, 1914.

TREASURES
OF THE SAHARAN
MANUSCRIPT
COLLECTIONS

In today's world, where satellite links and high-speed Internet connections mean messages can travel between continents almost instantaneously, and where scientists are experimenting with e-books, it is humbling to remember that in past centuries, men were so avid for knowledge that they would set out on a perilous journey across the desert just to consult a manuscript, copied by hand and passed down from generation to generation over hundreds of years. Traders were not the only people to cross the Sahara: men would set out in search of sources of spiritual wealth, traveling on foot from Oualata to Fez, Kairouan, or Mecca to meet fellow scholars, or to buy precious manuscripts for their own collection.

Naser ed-Din, the seventeenth-century Berber imam famed for his writings, advised his readers: "Every one of you, whenever you ride a horse, should carry a writing tablet in front of you, propped up by the pommel of your saddle, for there is no more shameful companion than ignorance for a man who hopes to cross the threshold of Eternity."

The oasis towns we have visited have been associated with scholarship for hundreds of years. In 1953, the historian Raymond Mauny noted down a foundation myth that recounted that in 542 A.H. (1147), three pilgrims from Mecca arrived in the Adrar region. Each wrote a letter and buried it in the sand, the first at Atar, the second at Chinguetti, and the third at Ouadane. A year later, they returned to dig them up again. They first went to Atar, but the letter had been swept away in a flood. The letter buried in Chinguetti was lost under the sands. The three pilgrims finally arrived in Ouadane, and there they found the letter buried a year before, with a few termite holes, but otherwise intact. It would be difficult to imagine a more charming tale accounting for the origin of three major centers of Islamic scholarship.

In centuries past, they were important centers of international scholarship, attracting men of letters, philosophers, and theologians from all over the Islamic world. Their flourishing

Cherîf Dade Ould Ydda in the courtyard of his home, discussing a manuscript with Balla Ould Abba.

Facing page: Cherîf Dade Ould Ydda's home is listed as a historic monument. Here, he is examining a manuscript written over three hundred years ago. His collection—one of the biggest in Tichit—contains manuscripts on a wide range of subjects, including religion, geography, history, the natural sciences, medicine, and so on.

Preceding pages: The Mohamedou Ould Baba family live in a tent in Tichit. On the left is Minatou, keeper of the manuscripts, which are stored in wooden chests. At the back of the tent a shakebou, *or traditional piece of nomad furniture, can be seen.*

trade economies and their location on the trans-Saharan caravan routes undoubtedly played a large part in establishing their reputations as intellectual centers. Some of the oasis towns have collections of manuscripts to rival any of the world's great libraries. For example, Tichit has literally hundreds of manuscripts on an incredible range of subjects, held by local families who act as guardians of this priceless cultural heritage. In Ouadane, the collection held by Mustafa Uld Khetta consists of over eighty manuscripts, the oldest of which dates back to the thirteenth century. The Ouadane mosque has three treatises on Sharia law written by women. The Habott family's house in Chinguetti holds one of the richest collections in the whole Sahara region—nearly 1,200 works, including one dating back to 480 A.H. (1085), covering subjects as diverse as logic, grammar, or abstruse points of Islamic jurisprudence.

These works were either written by scholars staying in these towns, or from the ninth century, imported from Egypt, Hijaz, or Palestine. They represent an infinitely precious resource, not just because of their value for collectors or their unparalleled interest for historians of Islamic thought and society, but because they represent the collective memory of the people of the Sahara, of Mauritania, and of Chinguetti itself. To take but one example,

the famous illuminated manuscript of the Koran known by the name *Bu'Aïn çafra* (the one with the yellow eye) in reference to a gold circle on the cover, is unique. It was on this golden "eye" that Ahmed Mahmud, the town's former *qadi* or magistrate, made witnesses swear to tell the truth. The binding of one ancient manuscript of the Koran, also held in Chinguetti, tells another story; it still bears the traces of the gold coins hidden there by Sheikh Uld Habott during his pilgrimage to Mecca. He chose the safest of hiding places, as no robber would dare to profane or defile such a sacred book.

There are estimated to be over forty thousand Arabic manuscripts in the two hundred and sixty or so collections in Mauritania alone. Mali likewise has a number of extraordinary collections, such as the Abdelkader Haïdara library, discovered early in 2000 by the Malian researcher Ismael Diadé Haïdara. This fabulous collection includes some three thousand Arabic manuscripts, the oldest written in the fourteenth century. It was started by the father of Mahmud Kati, author of the famous work on West African history called *Tarikh al-Fettash*. Mahmud Kati's father was himself a scholar, born in Toledo in Spain. He was exiled in Mali in 1468. Since then, the successive generations of the same family have been adding to this wonderful collection. It has been shown that strong cultural links were established between the Mauritanian oases and the town of Timbuktu very early on. In the days of the empire of Mali (from the early thirteenth century to the late fifteenth century), several scholars from Oualata held religious functions in Timbuktu, including the post of *qadi* (magistrate).

Thanks to the number of manuscripts in circulation, the intellectual and cultural life of the oases was highly developed. Masters would hold classes in their homes, while the mosques—especially in Oualata—organized debates on arcane points of Islamic theology. The oases have a proud and ancient tradition of ensuring knowledge was handed down through the generations. The earliest school in Tichit, for example, was founded in 536 A.H. (1141).

Unfortunately, these fabulous manuscript collections are under threat from a number of factors. The gradual decline in prosperity of the oasis towns, together with the relentlessly harsh climate, means the buildings where they are housed are in very poor condition, and the fragile manuscripts themselves in danger from sand, insects, and careless handling. There is also a desperate shortage of trained librarians. The most precious manuscripts are stored on open shelves, or bundled in trunks. Only twenty years or so ago, it was fairly common to enter a crumbling house in some abandoned oasis in the central Sahara and find the floor strewn with manuscripts hundreds of years old. Most of these have been lost forever. However, in 1979, UNESCO launched a campaign to preserve the unique cultural wealth of Chinguetti, Tichit, Ouadane, and Oualata, placed on the list of World Heritage Sites. This brought the subject to the attention of the international community, and in 1993 the Mauritanian government created the National Foundation for the Preservation of the Ancient Towns of Mauritania. Since then, a series of international conferences have been organized to discuss the best way to preserve this cultural heritage. In Chinguetti, the Ehel Habott Foundation has pledged to pay a quarter of the cost of restoring the town's manuscripts before they are scanned and made available on-line. The International Saharan Studies Research Center in Paris is preparing a dual-language (Arabic and French) anthology in several volumes of desert manuscripts from Mauritania, Mali, Niger, Morocco, Algeria, Tunisia, Libya, Egypt, Nubia, and Sudan. To give an idea of the size of this undertaking

and the importance of the cultural heritage saved from destruction, the researcher Ulrich Rebstock, working on a project run jointly by the Albert Ludwig University in Freiburg, Germany, and the Mauritanian Institute for Scientific Research, has begun a *History of Moorish Literature* that is to include over five thousand authors and some fifteen thousand titles. If this knowledge were allowed to vanish, the world's cultural heritage would be deeply impoverished.

The manuscripts lovingly copied by generations of scribes and scholars in far-flung reaches of the Sahara are now being recorded for posterity in new editions, on microfilm, and in Internet libraries. In the words of an old Arabic saying, "The quill is a cypress in the garden of wisdom; its shadow lengthens on the dust."

An exegesis of the Koran in the Mohamedou Ould Baba library in Tichit.

Facing page, top: *An exegesis of the Koran dating from c. 500 A.H. (c.1105), held in the Habott library in Chinguetti.*

Bottom: *A leather book cover stamped with metal, held in the imam's library in Oualata.*

The shelves of the Association for the Protection of Chinguetti's Historic Monuments hold many treasures, including ancient leather-bound volumes (facing), an old tablet inscribed with verses from the Koran that would have been used for teaching in a Koranic school, and a wooden ink pot (above).

The master of the Koranic school reading a manuscript.

Facing page: *Cherîf Dade Ould Ydda piecing together fragments of a number of manuscripts destroyed in the torrential rains that caused extensive damage and claimed a number of lives in the Tichit region in summer 1999. It would be a tragedy were this cultural heritage to be lost forever, but funds to rescue and restore the manuscripts are in short supply.*

*Gaithi Ould Saydi is a student and a member of the
Association for the Protection of Chinguetti's Historic
Monuments. He is pictured with one of the association's
precious manuscripts.*

Al-Ahmed Mahmoud reading in the quiet atmosphere of the library near the Chinguetti mosque.

Following pages: *Folios from a nine-hundred-year-old manuscript held in the Habott library in Chinguetti. This magnificent work tells the story of Muhammad and the early history of Islam.*

مراد بن كعب بن لؤي بن غالب بن

The elaborately decorated
walls and pillars of the
Oualata library. Readers
consult centuries-old
manuscripts cross-legged on
the floor or leaning on the
cushions scattered against
the walls.

Preceding pages:
An illumination from
a manuscript in the
Oualata library. The
calligraphy in the central
rectangle gives the title
of the work, Kitab al-Hajj,
or the Book of Pilgrimages.

157

Close-up views of the paintings in one of the niches in the Oualata library, including a stylized representation of a young woman with long braids (above), above which are drawn figures reminiscent of those found in the muchemma' *medallions around the doorways of the town (facing page).*

Following pages: *Architectural designs on a double page taken from a work detailing the genealogy of Muhammad, held in the Habott library, Chinguetti. The right-hand page shows Mecca with the Ka'aba in the center and the minarets around the walls.*

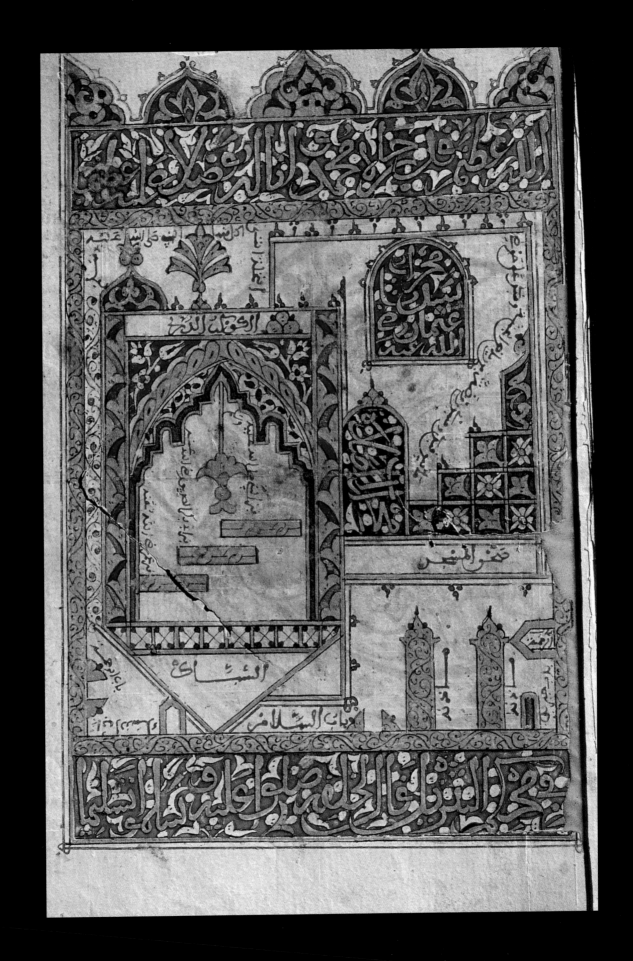

A *double-page spread from an exegesis on the Koran, held in the Habott library in Chinguetti.*

Preceding pages:
Left: *A page from an exegesis on the Koran held in Minatou Mohamedou Ould Baba's library in Tichit.*
Right: *Illuminations inspired by mosaics and architectural motifs in an exegesis on the Koran, held in the Habott library in Chinguetti.*

Following pages:
Left: *A page from an exegesis on the Koran, Oualata library.*
Right: *The title page from a copy of the al-Jami' al-sahih, a collection of Hadith (sayings) by the Prophet put together by 'Abd Allah Muhammad ibn Isma'il al-Bukhari, who lived in the ninth century. He was the earliest author to classify the Hadith by subject and to provide a detailed commentary. The manuscript is held in the Oualata library.*

سورة مريم عليها السلام مكية

بسم الله الرحمن الرحيم كهيعص ذكر
رحمت ربك عبده زكريا إذ نادى ربه نداء خفيا
قال رب إني وهن العظم مني واشتعل الرأس شيبا
ولم أكن بدعائك رب شقيا وإني خفت الموالي
من ورائي وكانت امرأتي عاقرا فهب لي من لدنك
وليا يرثني ويرث من آل يعقوب واجعله رب رضيا
يا زكريا إنا نبشرك بغلام اسمه يحيى لم نجعل
له من قبل سميا قال رب أنى يكون لي غلام وكانت

كتاب

الجامع الصحيح

للامام العلامة

ابي عبد الله محمد بن اسماعيل

الجعفي النجاري

THE COLORS
OF LIFE

Above: *A leather pouch used by the Fulani people of Niger for storing tobacco, sticks of antimony, and amulets.*

Above right: *A pair of traditional leather sandals hanging from a camel saddle belonging to a Niger Tuareg nomad in the Aïr desert.*

Facing page: *Berber women living in the Saoura oasis in Algeria tie their babies on their backs with brightly colored bolts of cloth.*

Preceding pages:
Left: *The interior of a* khaïmat, *or tent, near Boutilmit in the Mauritanian desert. The top of the patchwork canopy, propped up by two poles loosely tied together for ease of transport, is known in the Tagant region as "the eye of the tent."*

Right: *Saharan nomads use* menassa, *or metal bowls, for a wide variety of daily functions.*

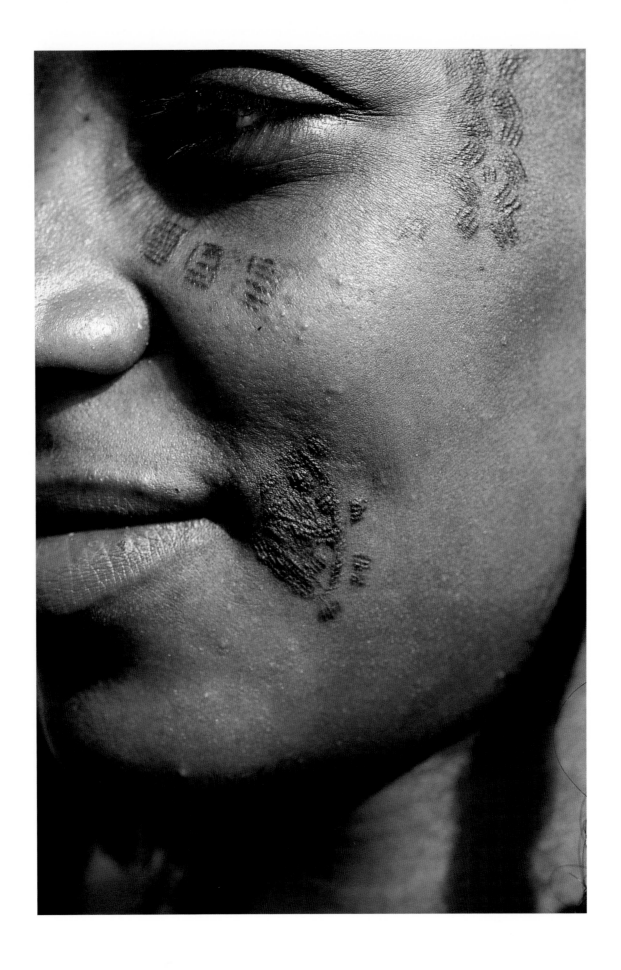

Women in the Mauritanian desert have traditionally
decorated their leather cushions and bags with natural
pigments. Nowadays, chemical pigments are often used.

Facing page: *Embroidery on a Fulani tunic from Niger.
The little circles symbolize* suudu, *or camps.*

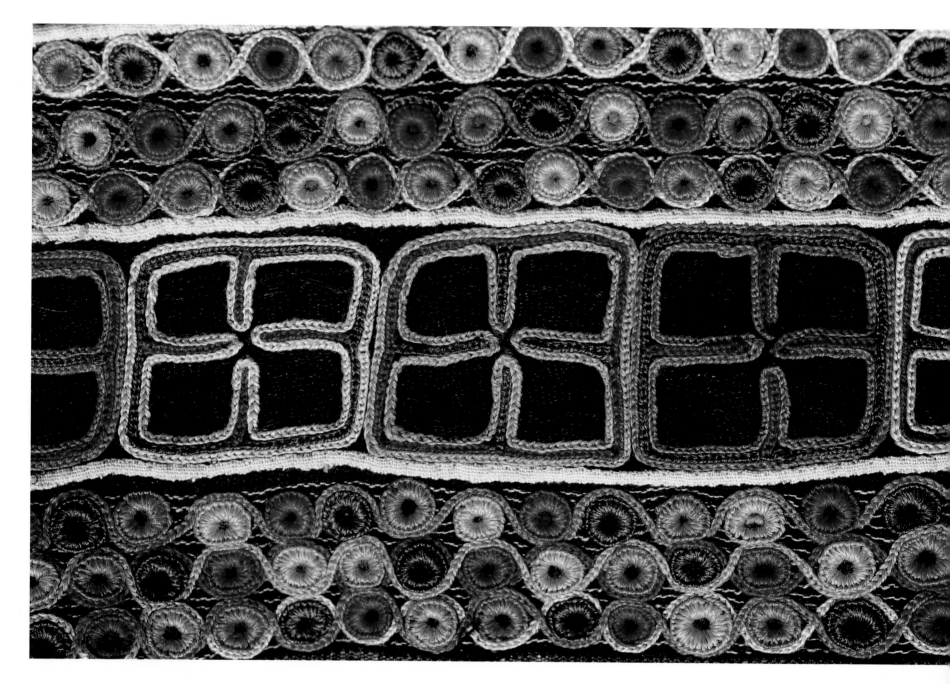

Preceding pages:
Left: *Facial tattoos are a ritual decoration for Fulani women.*
Right: *This young Fulani woman has braided cowry shells, glass and plastic beads, and bronze rings into her hair.*

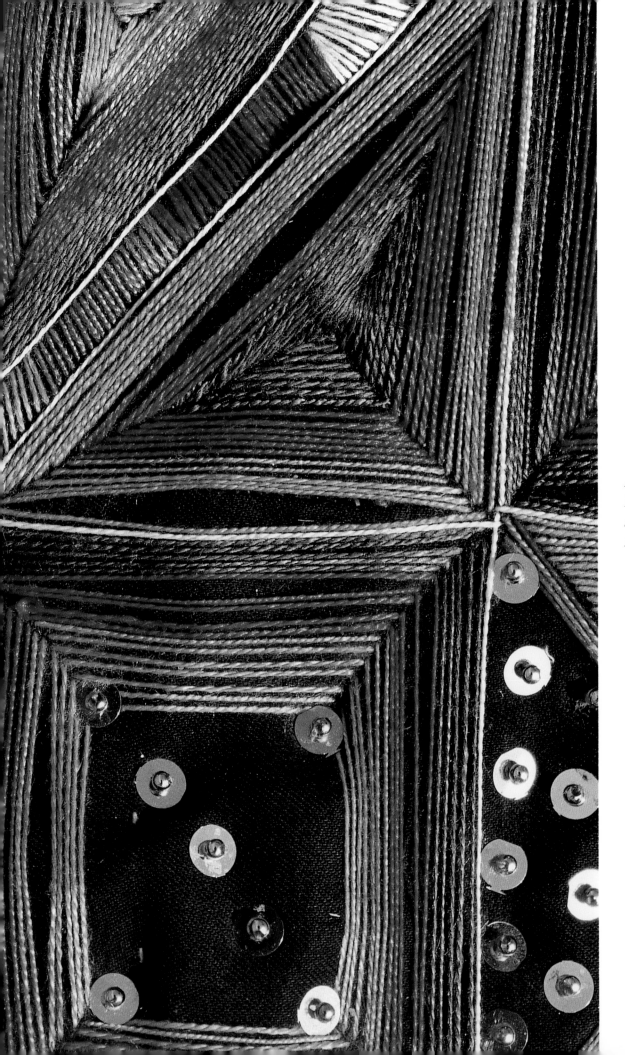

A richly embroidered throw for a camel saddle,
Niger. Tuareg camel drivers bring out these throws
at gatherings and festive occasions,
such as Mouloud.

Embroidered wool on the throw of a camel saddle, belonging to a Niger Tuareg in the Aïr desert.

This young Fulani woman is sheltering from
the sun under a brightly colored umbrella at
the great annual gathering to celebrate the
Worso festival.

*The brash scarlet of the chili pepper harvest in the
Saoura region of Algeria mirrors the softer red of a
calabash decorated by Fulani women in Niger.
These motifs are also used in facial tattoos.*

A close-up view of a wall in the
Baker's House in Agadez.

A camel-hair carpet in a tent belonging to Mauritanian nomads.

An air vent in a banco wall in Agadez.

This young Fulani man is made up ready to dance.
He has painted his lips black with a stick of antimony.

The semi-circles carved on this calabash symbolize the
Fulani suudu, *or campsite.*

This young Fulani man is now a Sukaabe—he is now mature enough to participate in the dances.

BIBLIOGRAPHY

Alexander, John. "The salt industries of West Africa: a preliminary study," in Thurston Shaw et al., *The Archaeology of Africa*. London: Routledge, 1993.

Amblard, Sylvie. *Tichit-Walata (R.I. Mauritanie). Civilisation et industrie lithique*. Recherche sur les Civilisations (Mémoire n° 35): Paris, 1984.

Barth, Heinrich. *Travels and Discoveries in North and Central Africa*. London: Frank Cass, 1965.

Bernard, Augustin. *Afrique septentrionale et occidentale. Sahara, Afrique occidentale*. Armand Colin: Paris, 1939.

Brookes, Geraldine. *Imazighen: The Vanishing Art of Berber Women*. London: Thames and Hudson, 1996.

Brosselard, Henri. *Voyage de la mission Flatters au pays des Touareg Azdjers*. Jouvet & Cie: Paris, 1883.

Bruce-Lockhart, J. and J. Wright, eds. *Difficult and Dangerous Roads: Hugh Clapperton's Travels in Sahara and Fezzan (1822–25)*. London: Sickle Moon, 2000.

Cordell, Dennis. *Dar al-Kuti and the Last Years of the Trans-Saharan Slave Trade*. Madison, Wisconsin: University of Wisconsin Press, 1985.

Cuoq, Joseph. *Recueil des sources arabes concernant l'Afrique occidentale du VIIIe au XVIe siècle (Bilâd al-Sudan)*. CNRS: Paris, 1975.

D'Agostino, Charles. "La porte magique du Sahara." *Le Mercure Universel* (July–August 1933).

Devisse, Jean and C. Robert. *Tegdaoust III. Recherches sur Audaghost. Fouilles de 1960 à 1965*. Mémoires de l'Institut mauritanien de la Recherche scientifique: Paris, 1981.

Diolé, Philippe. *Le plus beau désert du monde*. Albin Michel: Paris, 1955.

Duchemin, G.-J. "À propos des décorations murales des habitations de Oualata (Mauritanie)." *Bulletin de l'Institut Français d'Afrique Noire XII* (1950): 1095–2012

Durou, Jean-Marc. *Sahara: the Forbidding Sands*. New York: Harry N. Abrams, 2000.

Ech-Chengguiti al-Amîn, El-Wasit. "Littérature, histoire, géographie, mœurs et coutumes des habitants de la Mauritanie." Translated by M. Teffahi. *Études mauritaniennes* 5 (1953).

Encyclopédie Berbère. s.v. "Agadez."

Fleming, Fergus. *The Sword and the Cross: the Conquest of the Sahara*. New York: Grove Press, 2003.

Fromentin, Eugène. *Between Sea and Sahara: An Algerian Journal*. Translated by Blake Robinson. Athens, Ohio: Ohio University Press, 1999.

Gabus, Jean. *Art nègre. Recherche de ses fonctions et dimensions*. À la Baconnière: Neuchâtel, 1967.

Gaudio, A. "Intervention du CIRSS au Colloque international sur le Patrimoine culturel mauritanien." *La Nouvelle Revue Anthropologique* (January 2000).

Herodotus. *The Histories*. Translated by Aubrey de Sélincourt. Harmondsworth: Penguin, 2003.

Hudson, Peter. *Travels in Mauritania*. London: HarperCollins, 1991.

Hugot, Henri J. and Maximillian Bruggmann. *Rock Art of the Sahara*. Paris: Vilo, 2000.

Ibn Battuta. *Travels in Africa and Asia 1325–1354*. Edited by H. Gibb. New Delhi: Low Price, 1999.

Jacques-Meunié, D. "Cités caravanières de Mauritaine : Tichite et Oualata." *Journal de la Société des Africanistes* 27 (1957): 19–35.

———. *Cités anciennes de Mauritanie. Province du Tagant et du Hodh*. Klincksieck: Paris, 1961.

Kennedy, Geraldine. *Harmattan: Journey Across the Sahara*. Santa Monica: Clover Park, 1994.

Laureano, Pietro. *Sahara, jardin méconnu*. Larousse: Paris, 1991.

Leclant, Jean. *Témoignages des sources classiques sur les pistes menant à l'oasis d'Ammon*. Institut français d'Archéologie orientale: Cairo, 1950.

———. "Oasis. Histoire d'un mot" in *À la croisée des études libyco-berbères, mélanges offerts à P. Galand-Pernet et L. Galand*. Geuthner: Paris, 1993.

Marozzi, Justin. *South from the Barbary: Along the Slave Routes of the Libyan Sahara*. London: HarperCollins, 2001.

Mauny, Raymond. "Niches murales de la maison fouillée à Koumbi Saleh." *Notes africaines* 46 (1950): 34–5.

———. "Notes d'histoire et d'archéologie sur Azougui, Chinguetti et Ouadane." *Bulletin de l'Institut Français d'Afrique Noire XVII* (1955): 142–62.

Miske, A. B. *Al-Wasit. Tableau de la Mauritanie au début du XXe siècle*. Klincksieck: Paris, 1970.

Monod, Théodore. "À l'Ouest du nouveau. Une exploration scientifique au Sahara occidental." *Sciences et Voyages XVII* (1936): 329–42.

———. "Sur quelques détails d'architecture africaine." *Acta tropica IV* (1947): 342–345, 1947.

———. "Sur quelques constructions anciennes du Sahara occidental." *Bulletin de la Société de Géographie et d'Archéologie de la Province d'Oran LXXI* (1948): 23–52.

———. *Méharées*. Actes Sud: Paris, 1989.

———. *Sahara: Magic Desert*. Santa Barbara: Arpel, 1989.

Monod, Théodore and Marc de Gouvenain. *Majâbat al-Koubrâ*. Actes Sud: Paris, 1996.

Monod, Théodore and Jean-Marc Durou. *Déserts*. AGEP: Marseille, 1998.

Nachtigal, Gustav. *Sahara and Sudan*. Translated by A. and H. Fisher. London: C. Hurst, 1974.

Nantet, Bernard. *L'invention du désert. Archéologie au Sahara*. Payot: Paris, 1998.

Porch, D. *Conquest of the Sahara*. Oxford: Oxford Paperbacks, 1986.

Puigaudeau, Odette du. *Tagant*. Julliard: Paris, 1949.

———. "Contribution à l'étude du symbolisme dans le décor mural et l'artisanat de Walâta." *Bulletin de l'Institut Français d'Afrique Noire XIX* (1957): 137–83.

———. "Architecture maure." *Bulletin de l'Institut Français d'Afrique Noire XXII* (1960): 92–133.

———. "Oualata : ville saharienne, un musée dans le desert." *Jeune Afrique* 167 (1964): 28–29.

———. *Pieds nus à travers la Mauritanie, 1933–1934*. Phebus: Paris, 1992.

Strabo. *Geography*. Translated by H. L. Jones. Cambridge, Mass.: Loeb, 1969.

Tolba, Anne-Marie and Serge Sibert. *Villes de sables. Les cités bibliothèques du désert mauritanien*. Hazan: Paris, 1999.

Vernet, Robert. *Préhistoire de la Mauritanie*. Centre culturel français A. de Saint Exupéry: Nouakchott, 1993.

Vikor, K. *The Oasis of Salt: A History of Kawar*. London: C. Hurst, 1999.

Villiers, Marc de and S. Hirtle. *Sahara: the Life of the Great Desert*. London: Harper Collins, 2003.

ACKNOWLEDGMENTS

The photographers would like to thank the following people:

Carla Milone.

In Niger: Alberto Nicheli and Transafrica; Mahoumoudan Ghaliou, whose expertise, culture, and humor we greatly appreciated, and his travel agency Air Voyages Niger in Agadez; Rissa Ag Boula, minister of tourism; and the director general of the Ministry of Tourism at Niamey.

In Mauritania: Ahmed Ould M'Deih and his travel agency Imraguen Tours for their logistic support and help on the ground; Abdhullah Ould Moubarek, Nabouhya Sidi, Lebat, Bilal, Bekai, and the guide Anani, for their untiring efforts.

We would particularly like to thank all those who allowed us to visit their libraries: in Tichit, Cherîf Dade Ould Ydda Ehmalla Ould, Balla Ould Abba, Minatou Ould Baba and Cherîf Ould Emehaned, Ahmedou Ould Najemme, and the mayor of Tichit; in Chinguetti, Al-Ahmed Mahmoud, Mohamed Goulham Habott, and Gaithi Ould Saydi; in Oualata, Taleb Boubakar and the imam of Oualata.

Thanks also to all those who welcomed us into their homes and allowed us to photograph them.

[1] Herodotus, *The Histories*, Aubrey de Sélincourt, trans. (Harmondsworth: Penguin, 2003).
[2] Arthur Rimbaud, "Flowerbeds of Amaranths," in *Collected Poems*, Oliver Bernard, trans. (Harmondsworth: Penguin, 1987).

Translated from the French by *Susan Pickford*
Copyediting: *Chrisoula Petridis*
Typesetting: *Octavo*
Proofreading: *Christine Schultz-Touge*
Color Separation: *Dupont Photogravure, Paris*

Originally published in French as *Tableaux du Sahara* © Arthaud, Paris, 2000
English-language edition © Éditions Flammarion, 2004

04 05 06 4 3 2 1

FC0433-04-IV
ISBN: 2-0803-0433-X
Dépôt légal: 04/2004

Printed in Italy by Canale